THE (no leftovers!) CHILD CARE COOKBOOK

Kid-Tested Recipes and Menus for Centers & Home-Based Programs

by Jac Lynn Dunkle and Martha Shore Edwards

Illustrations by Brian Barber

Redleaf Press
a division of Resources for Child Caring

Martha Shore Edwards is a freelance journalist with a degree in journalism from the University of North Carolina and an MBA from Vanderbilt University. She is the mother of three daughters, all of whom were cared for in centers directed by Ms. Dunkle. Their friendship and mutual interest in good nutrition for young children led to this cookbook.

Jac Lynn Dunkle has been director of the employee-sponsored center at Vanderbilt University since 1987. Her interest in nutrition springs from her commitment to improve all aspects of care for the young children in her programs. Ms. Dunkle is an accomplished trainer, currently doing workshops on nutrition for the Tennessee Department of Human Services and at NAEYC fall conferences.

© Copyright 1992 by Jac Lynn Dunkle and Martha Shore Edwards

Published by: Redleaf Press
a division of Resources for Child Caring
450 North Syndicate Suite 5
St. Paul, MN 55104

ISBN: 0-934140-64-2

Library of Congress Cataloging-in-Publication Data

Dunkle, Jac Lynn, 1951–
    The (no leftovers) child care cookbook: kid-tested recipes and menus for center & home-based programs/by Jac Lynn Dunkle and Martha Shore Edwards.
        p. cm.
    Includes bibliographical references and index.
    ISBN: 0-934140-64-2: $14.95
    1. Cookery. 2. Children–Nutrition. 3. menus. 4. Quantity cookery. I. Edwards, Martha Shore, 1952– . II. Title.
III. Title: Child care cookbook.
TX652.D86 1992   92-15973
641.5'7–dc20   CIP

Printed in the United States of America

This book is dedicated to

Audrey and John Hockaday,

Jac Lynn's parents

and

Eleanor Sue and Dick Shore,

Marty's parents

ACKNOWLEDGEMENTS

Hearty thanks to Ramona DeBoer who spent many hours reviewing the recipes for their compliance to the Child and Adult Care Food Program (CACFP) regulations and offered very practical suggestions based on her many years as Nutritionist with the CACFP program in Tennessee.

Thanks to Dr. Cathy Dundon, the Tennessee spokesperson for the American Academy of Pediatrics, for her enthusiasm about the book and her guidance in the nutrition and eating behavior chapters.

Thanks to Jill Hockaday Coble, Jac Lynn's sister, for her help in developing more nutritional recipes.

Thanks to Helen Andrews, the faithful cook at Vanderbilt Child Care Center, for her helpful suggestions and support.

And finally, thanks to our spouses, Gary Dunkle and Palmer Edwards, and our children, Audrey and Joann Dunkle and Julie, Emily and Susan Edwards, who spoke proudly about the cookbook and gave us moral support when we needed it most.

THE (NO LEFTOVERS!) CHILD CARE COOKBOOK

TABLE OF CONTENTS

INTRODUCTION TO THE (NO LEFTOVERS!) CHILD CARE COOKBOOK

The purpose of this cookbook is to promote the use of nutritious, tasty recipes for children who are fed meals and snacks in child care centers and family child care homes. Our focus is on children, from age one up to six years old, whose diets are not restricted. We want to reach children before they begin to make their own eating decisions and help them establish good eating habits.

This cookbook was developed with two groups of adults in mind – those who plan menus for young children and those who actually do the cooking. We hope to make menu planners better aware of the endless possibilities for making nutritionally-smart choices.

Many cooks want to plan more nutritious meals for children, but are lacking the expertise and/or management support. This book is an effort to address those needs.

Part One of the cookbook provides information you need to adapt your meals and snacks to be more nutritious for young children. Topics in Part One include the nutritional needs of young children and ways to develop a more nutritional approach to preparing meals and snacks in your home or center. Common questions parents have about picky eaters are addressed.

A special feature of the Child Care Cookbook is the straightforward explanation of the Child and Adult Care Food Program (CACFP). The CACFP, a United States Department of Agriculture program, offers nutrition support and financial assistance to cover food costs to child care centers and family child care homes. Every recipe in *The (No Leftovers!) Child Care Cookbook* is creditable under the CACFP, and includes all the information necessary to complete the CACFP production plan.

Part Two of the cookbook is a complete four-week cycle of menus and recipes, and additional recipes for entrees, snacks, and party foods. To save the cook time, all recipes are calculated for servings of 6, 20, 50 and 100 preschoolers. "Plan Ahead Tips" are included where appropriate and, whenever possible, items prepared from scratch are paired with quick-to-fix foods. All of the recipes have been child-tested in child care centers and family child care homes.

Jac Lynn is the director of the Child Care Center at Vanderbilt University, and Marty, a freelance writer, entrusted her three daughters to Jac Lynn's care for seven years. Both have experienced the development of these recipes and seen the children respond to them positively. The meals and snacks included in this book provide a varied diet that includes items from each of the major food groups. This kind of diet is recommended by the American Academy of Pediatrics (AAP) for children over one year of age as the best assurance of nutritional adequacy. Foods moderate in fat, salt, and sugar have been chosen including plenty of fruits, vegetables, and whole grains. Special care has been taken to include a vitamin A vegetable or fruit at least twice a week, a vitamin C vegetable or fruit daily, and several iron-rich foods each day.

Evidence from the 1988 Surgeon General's Report on Nutrition and Health indicates that people who follow a diet incorporating the guidelines above will lessen their risk of developing chronic diseases such as coronary heart disease, some types of cancer, stroke, diabetes mellitus, and atherosclerosis. They will also be less likely to develop high blood pressure, obesity, dental diseases, osteoporosis, and gastrointestinal diseases. Although preschoolers are not at a high risk for these diseases, they will benefit in the long run by developing a taste for healthy foods.

Where appropriate, we have encouraged adherence to criteria for accreditation by the National Association for the Education of Young Children (NAEYC). Recipes from various cultures are included and caregivers are encouraged to follow guidelines that help children develop good eating habits.

There are many benefits to using these recipes and menus. Young children will acquire a taste for healthier foods. Parents, providers, and child care directors can feel satisfaction knowing that children are building healthy eating habits that significantly reduce their risk of chronic diseases. And child care centers and family child care homes will find it much easier to meet the requirements for CACFP funding if they use the menus we provide.

We hope this book will help you plan and prepare more nutritious meals for children in your center or home, and we hope your children will enjoy the recipes as much as ours do.

PART ONE

NUTRITION AND CHILD CARE

NUTRITION AND CHILD CARE

Part One of the cookbook supplies valuable information for adults who prepare meals and snacks for young children. We suggest you read these chapters before you begin to use the menus and recipes in Part Two. We think you will refer to these chapters often. Resources for further reading are provided in the Notes and Bibliography at the back of the book.

Chapter One is an overview of nutritional guidelines for young children *with recommendations for specific food choices and preparation techniques.* Recommendations are based on information obtained from the American Academy of Pediatrics, the American Heart Association, the American Dental Association, and the Surgeon General of the United States. This chapter is "must reading" for providers and parents who want to determine whether they are offering nutritious meals and snacks to their children.

Chapter Two is a step-by-step plan for changing the menus in a center or home to reflect the nutritional guidelines presented in Chapter One. Changing to more nutritional meal plans requires the cooperation of staff and parents. This chapter suggests how to organize the change to new menus and ways to involve staff and parents in the process.

Chapter Three addresses questions parents often have about children who are picky eaters or who seem to overeat.

Chapter Four explains the Child and Adult Care Food Program (CACFP), answers frequently-asked questions about CACFP, and gives instructions on how to complete a CACFP production plan. If you are not already a CACFP participant, the information will help you to understand the program requirements and determine whether it is worth your time to participate.

CHAPTER ONE

NUTRITIONAL NEEDS OF YOUNG CHILDREN
OR *"SHOULD I ADD A LITTLE BACON GREASE FOR FLAVORING?"*

Some child care providers feel comfortable as long as a hot lunch is served in their center or home each day. Hot dogs, fried chicken, and boxed macaroni and cheese are often favorites among children, and many providers are thankful when children eat whatever they are served.

It is not until you look closer at the nutritional content of these foods, and others that are commonly served, that you may become concerned.

Many foods prepared for children contain too much saturated fat, sugar, and salt, and not enough whole grains and vegetables. In the short run, children with poor diets may experience one or more of the following: fatigue and irritability, low resistance to illness, poor academic performance, obesity, and dental problems. As these children grow older, they will be at higher risk for developing chronic problems such as coronary heart disease, high blood pressure, stroke, and gastrointestinal disease.

The recipes and menus in this book are based on guidelines for good nutrition developed by the American Academy of Pediatrics (AAP), the American Heart Association (AHA), the U.S. Department of Agriculture (USDA), the Surgeon General of the United States, and the Child and Adult Care Food Program.

This chapter provides a summary of the nutritional guidelines which seem especially appropriate for young children. Also, specific food choices and food preparation techniques are discussed. These can help you revise some of your own favorite recipes to be as nutritional as possible.

National Nutrition Guidelines for Young Children

The AAP Committee on Nutrition recommends that children over one year of age have a varied diet that includes items from each of the major food groups – fruits and vegetables; breads and cereals; milk and dairy products; and meat, fish and eggs. Such a diet is the best assurance of adequate nutrition.[1]

The AAP Committee and its counterpart within the AHA encourage diets *lower in saturated fat* for children over two years old. Restricting fat in the diets of children under two years is not recommended.[2]

The reduction of saturated fat consumption in childhood helps reduce the risk of atherosclerosis and coronary heart disease in adulthood. Saturated fats are fats that usually harden at room temperature. They are found in animal products and in some vegetable products and they tend to raise the level of cholesterol in the blood. It is cholesterol which can build up as fatty deposits in the lining of the blood vessels and cause narrowing and scarring of the channels through which blood flows. Blockage of blood vessels can cause heart attacks and strokes.[3]

Lower rates of diverticulosis and some types of cancer are associated with diets that emphasize foods which are *high in complex carbohydrates and fiber* (whole grain cereals, breads, fruits, and vegetables). Consumption of foods with dietary fiber is also usually beneficial in the management of constipation and diverticular disease.[4] Although most of the beneficial effects of fiber refer to adults – the diseases mentioned require years to develop – the American Academy of Pediatrics recommends that children eat a substantial amount of fiber to ensure normal laxation. High-fiber, low-calorie foods should not be emphasized to the exclusion of other common food groups, however.[5] You can feel confident that the nutritional needs of children are being met if Child and Adult Care Food Program (CACFP) meal patterns for three to six year olds (shown on p. 37) are adhered to. All of the menus in this book were developed in accordance with CACFP guidelines.

The Surgeon General recommends *reducing sodium intake.* Studies have shown a relationship between high sodium diets and the occurrence of high blood pressure and stroke. Although young children are not at high risk for these diseases, a low-salt taste preference could be beneficial as children grow older and their risk for high blood pressure and stroke increases. Encouraging the appreciation of food prepared with flavorings other than salt can help children avoid developing the habit of salting their food.

Children's consumption of foods high in *sugar should be limited.* Children are particularly vulnerable to cavities as new teeth erupt. Each time a child eats food that contains carbohydrates (sugar and starches), bacteria in the mouth produce acids that can destroy tooth enamel and cause cavities. The acid production continues for twenty minutes or more following a meal or snack. The more often children eat these foods, the more acid attacks they incur.[6]

Foods that are *good sources of iron* and foods that contain *vitamin C* are important in a child's diet. Vitamin C increases the likelihood that iron will be absorbed efficiently and should be a component of an iron-rich menu. Iron deficiency hampers the body's ability to produce hemoglobin, a substance needed to carry oxygen in the blood. When a child's brain does not get enough oxygen, the child feels tired and irritable and may be less resistant to disease and less able to perform academically. The Surgeon General has noted several groups that are at high risk for iron deficiency, including children of low-income families.

Nutritional Guidelines for Children One through Five

- Include items from each of the major food groups.
- Reduce saturated fat in diets for children over two.
- Include a substantial amount of fiber-rich foods.
- Choose foods relatively low in sodium and limit the amount of salt added in food preparation and at the table.
- Limit consumption and frequency of use of foods high in sugar.
- Include foods that are good sources of iron and vitamin C.

Table 1-1

Making Your Own Recipes More Nutritious

Informed food choices plus smart cooking techniques add up to more nutritious meals. A few simple changes in shopping and kitchen habits will go a long way toward improving the nutritional content of the meals and snacks you serve. Favorite recipes can be easily altered to meet the requirements of good nutrition; substituting frozen vegetables for canned may be all that is necessary in a particular recipe.

The following are some recommendations for implementing governmental and medical guidelines for good nutrition in your center or child care home.

Saturated Fat and Cholesterol

Choose foods that are low in fat. Vegetables, fruits, whole grain foods, fish, poultry, lean meats, and low-fat dairy products are good choices. Also, use food preparation methods that add little or no fat. Several reduced-fat cooking techniques are listed in Table 1-2.

The AHA recommends the following vegetable oils: safflower, sunflower, corn, partially hydrogenated soybean, cottonseed, sesame, canola, and olive.[7] Robert Kowalski, author of *Cholesterol and Children*, recommends using peanut oil for Chinese wok cooking, olive oil for Italian dishes and salad dressings, and safflower or sunflower oil for other general kitchen uses.

Avoid butter, bacon drippings (That's right, don't add a little bacon grease for flavoring!), ham hocks, lard, salt pork, meat fat and drippings, shortening, suet, and margarine. When you must use margarine, choose one which lists one of the vegetable oils recommended by the AHA as the first ingredient on the label, and with twice as much polyunsaturated as saturated fat.

Hydrogenated fats are fats and oils changed from their natural liquid form to become more solid, such as most margarine and shortening. The AHA recommends eliminating hydrogenated fats from the diet. Also, chocolate, coconut, coconut oil, palm oil, or palm kernel oil should be avoided. They resemble saturated fats.

Appropriate meats include chicken and turkey with the skin removed. Lean beef, veal, pork, and lamb are acceptable as long as the visible fat is trimmed. Fish and shellfish are also recommended. Eggs, often served as a protein in meals, should be limited to three per person per week.

Try recipes with dried beans, peas, lentils, peanut butter, or low-fat cheese instead of meat a few times a week. This provides variety and helps children develop a taste for nutritious alternatives to the usual meats. You will notice our menus contain at least one non-meat entree each week. Also, try combining small amounts of meat, fish, or poultry with rice or pasta in mixed dishes or casseroles.

Milk products containing 0 - 1% milk fat are recommended for children over two years old. Avoid cream of all kinds and nondairy cream substitutes made with coconut, palm, or palm kernel oil.

Reduced-Fat Cooking Techniques

1. Skim the fat off meat juices before adding to stews, soups, and gravies. Fat rises to the top and hardens when meat juices are chilled allowing for easy removal. Convenient, fat-separating pitchers are also available.
2. Instead of frying a food item, roast, broil, or steam it.
3. Season with non-fat seasonings.
4. Try using two egg whites instead of a whole egg in recipes.

Table 1-2

Fiber

Choose breads (wheat, rye, raisin, white) made with whole-grain or enriched flours. Cereals and pasta are fiber-rich, and almost all fruits and vegetables are good choices when you want to include more fiber in a menu. Some exceptions, which are high in fat, are coconuts, olives, and avocados. Many parents worry that their children will get fat if they eat too many starchy foods such as breads, cereals, pasta, and starchy vegetables. In moderate-sized portions these foods are not extremely high in calories. However, added fat and sauces, like margarine or cheese sauce, can increase the total calorie count and should be limited.

When choosing vegetables and fruits, remember, the Child and Adult Care Food Program, like the AHA, recommends frequent use of foods rich in vitamins A and C. Vitamin A strengthens the body's resistance to infection and prevents night blindness. Vitamin C promotes absorption of iron. Specifically, the CACFP recommends that meals include a vitamin A vegetable or fruit at least twice a week and a vitamin C vegetable or fruit daily. See Tables 1-3 and 1-4 for good sources of these important vitamins.

High Vitamin A Foods		
Vegetables		Fruits
Asparagus	Spinach	Apricots
Broccoli	Squash (winter)	Cantaloupe
Carrots	Sweet potatoes	Cherries, red sour
Chili peppers (red)	Tomatoes	Nectarines
Kale	Tomato juice, paste, or puree	Peaches (not canned)
Mixed vegetables	Turnip greens	Plums, purple (canned)
Peas and carrots	Vegetable juices	Prunes
Pumpkin		

Table 1-3

High Vitamin C Foods		
Vegetables		Fruits
Asparagus	Peppers, sweet	Cantaloupe
Broccoli	Potatoes, white	Grapefruit
Brussels sprouts	Spinach	Grapefruit juice
Cabbage	Sweet potatoes	Oranges
Cauliflower	Tomatoes	Orange juice
Chili peppers (red)	Tomato juice, paste, or puree	Raspberries
Collards	Turnip greens	Strawberries
Kale	Turnips	Tangerines
Okra		

Table 1-4

Sugar
The American Dental Association (ADA) recommends using moderation when serving foods that are high in sugar, and reducing the amount of time carbohydrates (sugar and starches) are in contact with teeth. The goal is to reduce the potential for tooth decay.

The following guidelines are adapted for young children from the ADA publication *Diet and Dental Health*:[8]

1. Select and use foods wisely. Learn to identify foods which are high in sugar. Labels of processed foods list ingredients in descending order, according to weight. Sucrose, glucose, maltose, dextrose, lactose, fructose, and corn syrup are all forms of sugar.[9] If sugar appears near the top of the list, you may want to serve it as only a part of a meal or you may choose to make the item from scratch.

2. Serve foods that contain carbohydrates as part of a meal rather than alone as a snack. Carbohydrates are less harmful to teeth when eaten with other foods. One reason for this may be that saliva production is increased during a meal. Saliva helps neutralize acid production and helps to clear food out of the mouth. Also, certain foods, such as cheese and peanuts, may be friendly to the teeth. Eating these foods along with, or after, foods that contain carbohydrates may help to counter the effects of the acids produced by the bacteria in plaque.

3. Limit the number of snacks each day. This will help children reduce the number of different times acid attacks their teeth.

4. Be aware of the physical characteristics of food. Foods such as raisins, dates, and dried fruits tend to stick to the teeth. Although we think of honey and molasses as being natural foods, they may be worse on teeth than refined sugars. Including a drink with sticky foods helps wash the sugar from the mouth.

5. Have children floss their teeth and brush with a fluoride toothpaste at least once a day.

See Table 1-5 for some practical tips to help you reduce the amount of sugar in the meals you serve.

Reducing Sugar in Your Menus
• Buy cereals that have less than 6 grams of sugar per serving. (Be sure to check for sugar in all its forms – sucrose, fructose, etc.)
• Buy canned fruit that is packed in water, fruit concentrate, or light syrup.
• Use less sugar in baking; a ratio of one part sugar to two parts flour works well.
• Require children to brush their teeth after meals.

Table 1-5

Salt

Processed foods provide about a third or more of the dietary sodium consumed by Americans. Another third is added by the consumer. A few simple changes in shopping and cooking habits can do much to reduce the salt in our diets.

Avoid foods processed or preserved with salt. Use frozen and fresh vegetables whenever possible to avoid the salt in canned vegetables. Use alternative flavorings such as herbs, spices, and lemon juice in the preparation of foods.[10] See our recipe for Spice Mix on page 142. And finally, be sure to remove the salt shaker from the table!

Iron

Iron intake can be improved by increasing consumption of iron-rich foods such as lean meats, fish, certain kinds of beans, iron-enriched cereals, and whole grain-products. The AHA reminds us that we need to be careful to get iron from foods that are low in saturated fat and cholesterol. Remember, too, the body makes better use of the iron in these foods if they are served with a good source of vitamin C. Also, cooking in an iron skillet increases the level of iron in the diet because iron is absorbed by the food as it cooks.[11]

The Child and Adult Care Food Program recommends including several iron-rich foods each day. Table 1-6 lists foods high in iron.

High Iron Foods

Vegetables		Fruits
Asparagus (canned)	Parsnips	Apricots (canned)
Beans - green, wax lima (canned)	Peas, green	Cherries (canned)
Bean sprouts	Potatoes (canned)	Dried fruits -apples, apricots, dates, figs, peaches, prunes, raisins
Beets (canned)	Sauerkraut (canned)	Grapes (canned)
Broccoli	Squash (winter)	
Brussels sprouts	Sweet potatoes	
Dark green, leafy– beet greens, chard, collards, kale, mustard, greens, parsley, spinach, turnip, greens	Tomato juice, paste, puree, sauce	
	Tomatoes (canned)	
	Vegetable juice (canned)	

Meat and Meat Alternates	Bread and Bread Alternates
Dried beans and peas	All enriched or whole-grain bread and bread alternates
Eggs	
Red meat	
Peanut butter	
Shellfish	
Turkey	

Table 1-6

Reducing Fat and Salt

Cooking from scratch and using fresh or frozen vegetables can significantly reduce the amount of fat and sodium in a menu. We have contrasted a typical child care lunch menu with one in which the items are made from scratch and the vegetables are fresh or frozen. You can see that there is a significant difference in the fat and sodium content.

Typical Child Care Menu

	Serving Size	Fat	Sodium
Battered Fish Sticks, frozen	4 sticks (2 oz)	14 g	560 mg
French fries, frozen	3 oz	5 g	45 mg
Canned French-style green beans	½ c	0 g	350 mg
Chocolate chip cookies (store bought)	2 cookies	7 g	70 mg
Totals		26 g	1,025 mg

More Nutritional Menu

Salmon cakes (p. 65)	2 oz	1 g	290 mg
Mashed potatoes	3 oz	1.2 g	25 mg
French-style green beans, frozen (p. 116)	½ c	0 g	75 mg
Pumpkin cookies (p. 89)	2 cookies	6 g	8 mg
Totals		8.2 g	398 mg

CHAPTER TWO

FIVE STEPS TO MORE NUTRITIONAL MENUS
OR "WHAT HAPPENED TO HOT DOGS, POTATO CHIPS, AND JELLO?"

Once you have a clear understanding of why it is important to make menus as nutritional as possible, you must make a plan for implementing the needed changes in your center or home. Changes must be made in your menus as well as in the way cooks, teachers, parents, and children think about food.

The following guidelines give you our ideas on how to accomplish these changes in your center or home.

1. **Learn about nutrition**
   ___ Read Chapter One in this book for a summary of important nutritional issues and recommendations from the American Academy of Pediatrics, the American Heart Association, the American Dental Association, and the Surgeon General. The information will provide you with a foundation of knowledge about nutrition.

2. **Adopt the meal plans presented in this cookbook, or analyze and rewrite the menus you currently use**
   ___ Review the rotating menus presented in this cookbook.
   ___ Decide which recipes you want to adopt and whether they could be substituted for items already on your menu.

   ___ Determine which of your menu items you want to replace and which you cannot change. Be careful not to change too fast. You may want to add unfamiliar items gradually.
   ___ Write a party policy for your center. (See p. 166 about party policies for good nutrition.)

3. **Educate yourself, staff and administration and encourage support**
   ___ Work closely with the cook to ensure understanding of the menus and party policy. Discuss why you want to change the menus and be sensitive to the cook's concerns, if any. Explain that incorporating more nutritional ways of cooking may take more time at first, but the benefits to the children will be worth the changes that are made. Incorporate the cook's suggestions where possible.
   ___ With help from the cook, plan a staff meeting to introduce the new menus. Serve a variety of the foods on the menus and make sure everything is sampled. Discuss reasons for changing the food program. Analyze old and new menus and explain why the new menus are better. Go over each menu item and explain what is in it. Review the new party policy.

____ Explain the need for teachers to show support while they are eating with the children. Teachers should talk positively about the food being served while they are with the children.

Tips for Teachers and Caregivers

- **Do not salt your food while at the table with children or let them see you salt your food.**
- **Eat at least a small serving of every food served to the children.**
- **Eat only what the children eat. Do not eat chips, candy, or other food that is not on the menu. Of course, teachers or caregivers may eat what they want when on break or away from the children.**

____ Establish a time for teachers to give their feedback on the menus after all items have been served twice. If your menus repeat monthly, the meeting should be scheduled during the third month. In general, do not take an item off the menu if only one teacher says a class will not eat it. Go with the majority in order to maintain a variety of nutritional meals. Consider conducting a plate waste analysis (measuring the food that is thrown away) to verify which items are not being eaten, then determine why the food is not popular.

4. **Communicate with parents**
____ Plan a strategy for presenting the new menus and party policy to the parents. One approach is to announce in writing that the center or family child care home is incorporating a more nutritional menu and party policy and invite parental involvement in reviewing menu items. Give parents copies of the new menus and party policies. Encourage parents to visit the center or your home for lunch during the next two months and give feedback on the meals, or have an open house and serve a sampling of new menu items.

5. **Implement, evaluate, and revise the new menus**
____ Use up and replace items that have unnecessary fat, salt, sugar, and preservatives, or which lose much of their nutritional content through processing. Table 2-1 lists some items you may have on your shelf and ways to handle them.
____ Plan shortcuts for each week's menus and decide which items can be prepared ahead of time. Make sure you have biscuit mix and spice mix on hand (recipes provided on p. 142).
____ Implement your new meal plans. If you hear criticisms, remind staff that the menus will be evaluated at the scheduled meeting time after all meals have been served at least two times.

Improving Ingredients

Applesauce with sugar	Use in applesauce hermit recipe, page 82. Restock with applesauce that has no sugar added.
Beef fat	Discard beef fat. Restock with recommended vegetable oils (p. 16) or shortening.
Bleached white flour	Add enriched or whole-grain flour to your pantry. Enriched and whole-grain flour can be combined using a 50-50 mix. This will increase the amount of fiber and nutrients in the diet without significantly changing the flavor or texture of baked goods.
Canned soups	Use only in non-soup recipes. When serving soup as an entree, make the soup from scratch. This will allow you to control the amount of salt in the soup.
Canned vegetables	Use in soup or serve as is until gone. Be sure to drain and rinse canned vegetables to cut the salt. Restock with frozen or fresh vegetables to reduce salt in diet.
Store-bought cookies	Serve with fresh fruit, yogurt, or other nutritional item until used up. Make cookies from scratch to control the amount of sugar and salt.
Fruit with heavy syrup	Drain heavy syrup and rinse fruit before serving. Restock with fruit packed in fruit concentrate, light syrup, or water. This will help reduce the amount of sugar being served.
Jello/pudding mixes	Use up Jello in combination with homemade gelatin. Discard pudding mix or use up what you have. (Jello and pudding mix are not a CACFP reimbursable food.)

Table 2-1

_____ Evaluate your menus at a meeting of staff and parents and be responsive to their concerns. Do not change your menu, however, if only one class does not like an item. For example, older children may not like the cheese pizza at first because it isn't round like a take-out pizza, but younger children may eat it readily. Once they get used to the shape, even older children admit it is a favorite.

In the child care programs where these menus are now regularly used, the entire changeover took almost one year. The group most reluctant to change their established eating patterns was the five-year-old class. The four-year-old class was somewhat reluctant. By the time the fives had "graduated" to kindergarten and the fours took their place in the five-year-old class, all the children ate wonderfully. Now the programs prepare 1½ times the required food because the children eat so well.

CHAPTER THREE

EATING PATTERNS OF YOUNG CHILDREN

OR ""WHAT DO I DO WITH LITTLE JACK SPRAT AND HIS WIFE?"

Caregivers and parents sometimes worry about children's eating behaviors. They fear one child is not eating enough to stay healthy or that another child (who eats heartily) will become overweight.

What is Normal?

The American Dietetic Association and pediatricians and authors Barton D. Schmitt and Lydia Furman provide some indicators of normal eating behaviors for children aged one to five:

1. **It is typical for a child's appetite to slow down significantly during the second year of life**. Dr. Schmitt explains that between one and five years of age many children normally gain only 4 or 5 pounds. This is in contrast to the 15 pounds a child probably gained during the first year of life. Children in this age range can normally go three or four months without gaining any weight. This slowdown in growth results in a reduced need for calories and a normal decline in appetite.[1]

2. **Preschoolers' appetites ebb and flow, and typically resume during growth spurts**. It is okay to let a child eat only enough to satisfy his/her hunger. If a child is developing and growing normally and you are providing a variety of healthful foods, you can be confident that the child isn't starving[2].

3. **Children (and adults) prefer some foods more than others.** It is okay if children do not eat certain foods as long as they are offered a variety of nutritious foods. Dr. Furman explains that no child needs to meet every dietary requirement every day. In fact, studies have shown that, if offered a variety of nutritious foods, children do select a balanced diet.[3] Dr. Schmitt adds, "There are no essential foods, just essential food groups."[4] Vegetables, for example, are in the same food group as fruits. If a child would rather eat cantaloupe one day and no broccoli, a parent should feel good that the child has had a good source of vitamins A and C.

4. **If a young child is growing normally and is active and healthy, she is probably eating an appropriate amount of food and does not need to diet**. Dieting can be dangerous for young children. If an infant's diet is restricted, the infant (under two years of age) can experience delayed growth and development.[5] Rather than restrict an overweight child's diet, physical activity should be encouraged.[6]

5. **Younger children often need five small meals a day because their stomachs have limited capacities.**[7] Thus, nutritious snacks should be a part of the daily meal schedule.

6. **By twelve months of age a child should start to learn how to use a spoon and should be completely self-feeding by fifteen months of age.**[8] This does not mean the child will be able to eat neatly. She will probably make a mess, but will enjoy the meal.

Encouraging Good Eating Habits

1. **Make mealtime a happy, social time**. Teachers and caregivers should sit with children and eat what the children are eating.

2. **Respect the food preferences and appetite of the child**. Serve children family-style, using a serving dish for each food item brought to the table. Respond to the wishes of the younger children if they indicate a preference or dislike for a particular food item. Let children (three years old and up) serve themselves. Don't worry if the children do not serve themselves a portion of everything offered. Do not insist that children finish everything on their plate. Never punish a child for not eating.

3. **Don't give in to children who do not want to eat the healthy foods offered to them. Offer children only foods that are on the menu that day**. Do not go through the kitchen looking for something for a child to eat if she does not want what is served.

Try not to worry about the child. It's okay if she only eats one item or even no food at all at a particular meal. She will eat at the next snack or meal and, over time, will learn to like a variety of foods.

4. **Be as creative in food planning and serving as you are in planning for art projects**. Make sure menus include a variety of textures and colors.

5. **Include nutrition education in the curriculum**. Talk about food groups and where different foods come from. Let the children grow some foods. Tomatoes and herbs can be grown inside. Read stories about foods like *The Very Hungry Caterpillar* and *The Little Red Hen*.

6. **Get the children to help prepare foods for snacks and meals**. Children may be more inclined to eat foods they have a hand in preparing. Making Friendship Stew (each child brings something for the stew and you cook it) is a favorite activity among preschoolers. Children enjoy making pancakes and Peanut Butter Balls, too. Recipes for these activities are listed in the index.

7. **Educate parents about good nutrition**. Let parents of children in child care know what meals and snacks are planned each week. Encourage parents

to join their child for a meal at the center or in your family child care home and to talk to their children about good foods.

When to Worry

Dr. Schmitt recommends calling the child's physician regarding eating habits if:[9]
1. the child is losing weight.
2. the child has not gained any weight in six months.
3. the child has associated symptoms of illness (such as diarrhea or fever).
4. the child gags on some foods or vomits after eating.

The American Dietetic Association recommends asking a pediatrician or registered dietitian to evaluate the child's diet if the child rejects whole categories of food for more than two weeks.[10]

Always consult the child's pediatrician if you have other questions or concerns about eating behaviors.

Choking Hazards at Meal Time

Carefully monitoring children's eating patterns and behaviors can help us spot problems or potential problems. By paying attention during food preparation and mealtime, we can prevent food-related accidents and deaths from happening.

It is estimated that seventy-five children in America die each year as a result of choking on solid food. Most of these choking deaths occur in children who are less than four years old; with children under two years old at the greatest risk.[11]

Infants and young children sometimes do not grind or chew their food well and may attempt to swallow it whole. Choking occurs when food enters and blocks the airway (trachea). The food item prevents oxygen from getting to the lungs and brain. If the brain goes without oxygen for more than four minutes, brain damage or death may occur.[12]

The most dangerous foods are those that are round, smooth, firm, and about the size of the end of your finger or thumb.[13]

It is preferable to choose safe foods, but some potentially dangerous items can be prepared in a manner that makes them safe for young children to eat. (See Table 3-1.)[14,15] However, hard candy, peanuts, and raw carrots should never be served to children under four.

Preparing Food to Prevent Choking

Choking Hazard	Safe Preparation Technique
apples	slice in thin strips or cook
biscuits/cookies	choose soft types that will not break off in large, hard chunks
carrots	slice lengthwise and steam or grate
grapes	slice lengthwise in quarters
hot dogs	slice lengthwise in quarters
meat chunks	serve well-cooked, shredded strips of meat
peanut butter	do not serve spoonfuls; spread thinly on bread
popcorn	remove partially-popped and uncooked kernels
raisins	serve cooked in breads or casseroles for children under three

Table 3-1

At least one adult should eat with the children at all meals and snacks, to make sure they are seated while eating and drinking. Children should never eat while running or playing. Adults can encourage children to take small bites and chew food completely before swallowing. Children should never be forced to eat or swallow anything.

No matter how careful you are, children may still choke. In many cases, the child can dislodge an item by coughing and there is no need to intervene. However, teachers need to know when and how to administer first aid for choking. At least one teacher, certified in cardio-pulmonary resuscitation (CPR), should be on the premises at all times. The American Red Cross offers courses in child and infant CPR and first aid in child care settings.

The American Academy of Pediatrics (AAP) offers a brochure, *Choking Prevention and First Aid for Infants and Children*, and a chart, *AAP First Aid Chart*, which include instructions and diagrams to demonstrate how to help a choking child. You can order an AAP publications catalog from the American Academy of Pediatrics, Publications Department, P.O. Box 927, Elk Grove Village, IL 60009-0927. Their toll free number is 1-800-433-9016 (1-800-421-0589 in Illinois).

In summary,
- Keep foods which may cause choking away from children until they are four years of age.
- Prepare potentially dangerous food in a manner that will make the food safe for young children.
- Supervise children closely when they are eating.
- Know what to do if a child chokes.

CHAPTER FOUR

CHILD AND ADULT CARE FOOD PROGRAM
OR "HOW HARD IS IT TO GET REIMBURSEMENTS?"

The Child and Adult Care Food Program (CACFP) is a federal program of the Food and Nutrition Service of the U.S. Department of Agriculture (USDA). The primary goal of the CACFP is to improve the diet of children twelve years of age and younger. In 1990, the program changed its name from Child Care Food Program to include adults in day care.

The CACFP gives financial assistance to public and private non-profit organizations providing licensed or approved non-residential child care services in the United States. Organizations participating in the CACFP include, but are not limited to, day care centers, family child care homes, and institutions providing day care services for children who have handicaps. Also, private, for-profit centers that receive compensation under Title XX of the Social Security Act for at least 25 percent of the children who are receiving non-residential day care may qualify as eligible child care institutions. Centers can operate the CACFP either independently or under the auspices of a sponsoring organization. Sponsoring organizations can operate the program in day care centers, outside-school-hours care centers, and family child care homes. The sponsoring organization must accept full administrative and financial responsibility for centers and homes under its auspices. Family child care homes must participate under a sponsoring organization (usually called a food program); they cannot enter the CACFP directly.

CACFP financial assistance comes in the form of a reimbursement for money spent by family child care homes and child care centers for approved meals and snacks. The CACFP can provide reimbursement for up to three meals per day. If three meals are served, at least one of them must be a snack. The daily menus in this book include breakfast, lunch/supper, and snack.

The CACFP specifies meal patterns (the inclusion of certain food groups at each meal) and minimum portion sizes. Table 4-1 gives meal pattern requirements for children three through five years old. We use these portions, even though our menus are for 1 and 2 year olds also, in order to keep meal planning simple when cooking for children of different ages. Children under the age of three may eat slightly larger servings than required by the CACFP, but they eat the portions with no adverse effects and we rarely have leftovers.

CACFP Meal Patterns for Children Three through Five Years Old

Breakfast

Milk, fluid	¾ cup
Juice or **fruit** or **vegetable**	½ cup
Bread and/or **cereal**, enrided or whole-grain	
Bread or	½ slice
Cereal: Cold, dry or	⅓ cup [or ½ ounce (weight), whichever is less]
Hot, cooked	¼ cup

Snack

Serve two of the following four foods. Juice may not be served when milk is served as the only other food.

Milk, fluid	½ cup
Meat or **meat alternate**	½ ounce
Juice or **fruit** or **vegetable**	½ cup
Bread and/or **cereal**, enriched or whole-grain	
Bread or	½ slice
Cereal: Cold, dry or	⅓ cup
Hot, cooked	¼ cup

Lunch or Supper

Milk, fluid	¾ cup
Meat or **meat alternate**	
Meat, poultry, or fish, cooked (lean meat without bone)	1½ ounces
Cheese	1½ ounces
Egg	1
Cooked dry beans and peas	⅜ cup
Peanut butter	3 tablespoons
Vegetable and/or **fruit**, two or more	½ cup total (juice cannot be counted for more than ½ requirement)
Bread or **bread alternate**, enriched or whole-grain	½ slice

Note: The USDA Food and Nutrition Service provides a detailed list of meat and bread alternates in the *Food Buying Guide for Child Nutrition Programs*.

Table 4-1[1]

Much of the following information about the CACFP applies to child care centers. **If you are a family child care provider, the requirements for your participation in the CACFP will probably be simpler and use fewer forms.** Whether you are in a center or family child care home however, remember that the CACFP is a federal program administered through the states and requirements will differ in each state. You must contact your local CACFP representative for local guidelines.

QUESTIONS ABOUT CACFP

How can I get more information about CACFP?

A: Call your local CACFP representative and ask for CACFP guidelines and an application. If you do not know who your CACFP representative is, call the regional office of the USDA Food and Nutrition Service. A list of regional offices is provided on p. 186.

What is involved in the application process and how long does it take to complete?

A: The application asks you to answer questions about your program — hours of operation, days per week, etc. It also asks what you do to include low-income families in your program and how you advertise your program in "grass-roots" areas. You are asked about the ethnic makeup of the children you serve. The child care program must operate in accordance with USDA policy which does not permit discrimination because of race, color, national origin, sex, religion, or handicap.

After an application is completed, a CACFP monitor schedules a visit to the program to observe a meal being served. The monitor is looking for adherence to CACFP guidelines concerning serving sizes, food components, and the cleanliness of the food preparation area.

The total time getting approval should not take more than two months.

What paperwork is required once you begin participating in the program?

A: Each month, the child care facility must provide the following information (reimbursements are made based on this information) on a reimbursement form:

- Total attendance for entire center or home
- Total servings of meals by type for which reimbursement is claimed
- Current monthly enrollment by eligibility category
- Total operating days in the month

In addition, the facility must maintain the following records for three years (these may be inspected by the CACFP):

- Production plans for meals and snacks served (not a requirement for family child care homes)
- Master roster of children enrolled
- Grocery receipts
- Monthly milk inventory
- Applications for free or reduced meals from eligible families (not a requirement for family child care homes, except provider's own children).

How much time does it take to do the paperwork required by CACFP?

A: If the child care facility adheres to the menus provided in this cookbook, center staff or provider could expect to spend a total of thirty minutes each day preparing all CACFP information. This includes production plans which are the most time-consuming, but are required of child care centers only.

How much money can a child care facility expect to receive from CACFP?

A: The amount of money reimbursed to a child care center or home depends on the number and income level of the children attending the program and the number of meals or snacks served. There are three levels of reimbursement for child care centers: 1) Free, 2) Reduced, and 3) Paid.

A child care center serving fifty children breakfast, lunch or supper, and a snack in fiscal year 1991 received an average monthly reimbursement as follows:

Free $3339
Reduced $2363
Paid $ 557
(These monthly reimbursements assume all children fit into the category noted and all children are present for every meal and snack, five days a week.)

The reimbursement rate for family child care homes is the same for children of all income levels. In a child care home with six children, the average monthly reimbursement would have been $331 in Fiscal Year 1991. (This assumes all children were present for two meals and a snack, five days a week.)

Our program is in an area that serves primarily middle and upper-income families. Are we still eligible to receive funds even if we have no children in the free or reduced category?

A: As long as a program does not discriminate, is public or private nonprofit, strives to publicize the program to low-income families, and serves food according to CACFP guidelines, the program can receive funds.

If we are approved to receive funds and our program serves families in middle and high income levels, would we be taking money from programs that need the money more?

A: To date, no qualifying program has been turned down because of a lack of funds. Each year that you renew your contract, we advise you to ask this question of your CACFP monitor.

The primary goal of the CACFP is to improve the diet of children twelve years of age and younger. Even if your program doesn't necessarily need the funding, you may see the need for improvements in your current menu after reading this cookbook. The CACFP funds could offset the expense incurred for providing more nutritious foods for your children or allow you to pay someone to prepare foods from scratch. Fresh fruits, cheese, fresh baked items and 100% fruit juice cost a little extra but can improve the nutritional content of your menus.

Nutrition is an important part of good health. Proper nutrition is also an important part of a good child care program.

Our program only serves two snacks and the children bring their own lunch. Can we receive funds just for snacks?

A: If you serve snacks according to standards, you can be reimbursed for up to two snacks per day.

What is a production plan?

A: Production plans indicate what food was served to whom (children and teachers) each day. The CACFP specifies what food components should be included in each meal or snack as well as how much of each component should be served. (See Table 4-1.)

The Production Plan

The following is a step-by-step explanation of how to fill out a Production Plan. The daily menu we used as an example is provided in this cookbook for Monday, Week One, p. 51 and is shown again in Figure 4-1.

MONDAY	
Menu Item	**Serving Size=Requirement**
Breakfast	
Toast, thin-sliced bread	1 slice = 1 bread
Mandarin oranges, canned	½ c = 1 fruit
Milk, fluid	¾ c = 1 milk
Egg Puff (optional)	1 Egg Puff = ½ meat
Lunch/Supper	
Chili	¾ c = 1 meat; ½ fruit/vegetable
Baked apple	¼ c (or ½ whole apple) = ½ fruit/vegetable
Corn bread	1 serving = 1 bread
Milk, fluid	¾ c = 1 milk
Snack	
Graham crackers (5 x 2½")	1½ crackers = 1 bread
Juice, 100% fruit	½ c = 1 fruit

One serving of chili contains meat (½) and beans (½) to equal one full meat requirement.

Figure 4-1

The completed production plan (Figure 4-2) for the State of Tennessee is similar to what you will find in most states. You should contact your local CACFP representative to obtain the production plan form for your state.

Item (1)   Name of center.

Item (2)   Date food served.

Item (3)   Number of children and adults actually served. You should fill in the number of children served immediately upon service. Adults should be served child-size portions.

Item (4)   Menu. Include the whole menu in detail. Note that milk must be listed as "Milk, fluid" every time it is served. You must indicate the specific juice or fruit served. In some of our menus we have indicated just "Fruit in season" or "Fruit juice" so that you can choose the fruits that are available and reasonably priced. Just remember, any time you substitute an item in your standard menu, be sure to indicate it on the Production Plan.

List all menu items in Item (4) even if they are optional (such as the Egg Puff in this instance). Optional components will not affect the rate of reimbursement.

Figure 4-2   (1) CACFP Food Production Plan for the Vanderbilt Child Care Center in Tennessee   (2) Date _____

	(3) Number of meals served by age.	(4) MENU	(5) FOOD ITEMS	(6) Portions Plan'd Size (a)	Number (b)	(7) Quantity of Food Purchased Units (2)	Actually Served (b)	Leftover (c)
BREAKFAST	1 - 2 _____ 3 - 5 __44__ 6 - 12 _____ Adults __4__	Egg Puff Oranges Toast Milk, fluid	(Optional) Canned, light syrup Whole wheat, thin-sliced 2% Fluid milk	1 piece ½ cup 1 slice ¾ cup	50 50 50 50	 2–#10 Cans 50 slices 2½ gallons	same as plan	none
AM SNACK	1 - 2 _____ 3 - 5 _____ 6 - 12 _____ Adults _____							
LUNCH	1 - 2 _____ 3 - 5 __45__ 6 - 12 _____ Adults __4__	Chili w beef & beans Baked apples Corn bread* Milk, fluid	¾ cup = Beef, 30% fat Kidney beans Tomatoes, canned Apples, canned *Recipe on file 2% Fluid milk	¾ oz beef ³⁄₁₆ c beans ¼ cup ¼ cup 1 piece ¾ cup	50 50 50 50	3# gr beef #10 can beans 1–#10 can tomatoes 2–#10 can apples 2½ gals. milk	same as plan	none
PM SNACK	1 - 2 _____ 3 - 5 __45__ 6 - 12 _____ Adults __10__	Graham crackers Juice, apple	Honey Grahams, enriched 100% juice made from concentrate	3–2"x 2" ½ cup	50 50	2½ lbs 3 gal & 1 quart	Served 55 3 lbs crackers 3½ gal juice	none
SUPPER	1 - 2 _____ 3 - 5 _____ 6 - 12 _____ Adults _____							

When you adhere to the menus in this book, this column will not change. It can be filled out, copied, and used each time this menu is served (every 4th week on Monday).

Item (5) Food Items. List the food items that make up the menu in Item (4). Line up food items with menu items straight across the form. Be sure to describe food items completely using the required format, i.e., "toast, whole-grain, thin-sliced" and "ground beef, 30% fat."

Item (6a) Portions Planned — size. This is where you show how each food contributes to the required component at a meal. Refer to Table 4-1 for required components.

Where we have specified one meat as the requirement, you can assume that the meat in the recipe provided 1½ ounce. If eggs, cheese, beans, etc. also contribute to the meat requirement, we will specify this.

A full bread requirement is ½ ounce.

Most of our recipes indicate serving size, but in some instances it is listed as "l serving = l___ ." It is your responsibility to measure the serving size, either by measured inch, weight, or measuring cup. In most instances we have done this for you.

Note that a combination of foods meeting a requirement must be listed by components. Chili has both beef and kidney beans meeting parts of the meat requirement. It is listed as "¾ ounces beef" and "³⁄₁₆ cup beans." A ¾ cup serving of chili will have those amounts in each serving. The chili is also meeting ½ of the fruit/vegetable component.

Item (6b) Portions Planned – number. Indicate how many people for whom each food item is being prepared. In a program of fifty children, usually not all fifty are there for breakfast. You can take an average and prepare for that many or you can prepare for fifty and measure the leftovers (Item 7c).

If teachers or other adults are eating breakfast, they must be included in this item. They should be served child-size portions. However, you may not claim adults for reimbursement.

Item (7a) Quantity of Food–Purchased Units. List items actually purchased (or used) to make this menu. You must use the *Food Buying Guide for Child Nutrition Programs* to calculate how much food is needed for this menu to meet the requirements. The guide is published by and available from the USDA Food and Nutrition Service.

Our sample production plan is completed for fifty servings. Therefore we have purchased or used enough food to meet the portion requirements for fifty people. At breakfast, we used fifty slices of thin sliced bread which equals fifty servings of bread based on the ½ ounce requirement. Thin-sliced bread is the same as one-half of a regular slice of bread. We used two #10 cans of mandarin oranges based on the serving size of ½ cup of fruit, and used 2 gallons and 7 cups of milk based on the serving size of ¾ cup for each serving.

Since the Egg Puff is optional it is not necessary to indicate it here.

Item (7b) Quantity of Food–Actually Served. If you serve more than the number of people for which you planned, show the adjustments here. In our example, we actually served the afternoon snack to forty-five children and ten adults for a total of fifty-five. Note that we used more crackers and more juice to serve enough food to meet the program requirements.

If you have no changes to what you planned, write "Same as Planned."

Item (7c) Quantity of Food–Leftover. Indicate leftovers here, if any. Leftovers must be weighed or portioned out and can be labeled, dated, and refrigerated or frozen for use at a later date.

Leftover foods that have been served family style must be thrown away. Check with your local CACFP representative to find out more about rules governing family-style service. Write "None" if you have no leftovers.

As you can see, completing a production plan can be time-consuming. When you use *The (No Leftovers!) Child Care Cookbook* recipes, the time for completing the production plan is greatly reduced. You just use the information from the recipes to fill in the production plan. We have done the calculations and each recipe meets CACFP requirements.

PART TWO

MENUS AND RECIPES

MENUS AND RECIPES

Part Two, the heart of the cookbook, presents four weeks of menus and recipes that meet Child and Adult Care Food Program requirements, with additional recipes for entrees, side dishes, snacks, and party foods. (See Chapter Four for information on the CACFP.) If items on the menu are not part of a recipe, we have referred to the Quick Reference Chart on the inside front cover, last page and inside back cover, which will tell you the amount of the item to purchase and prepare. ﹖

In our menus, we use the minimum portions required by CACFP for children age three through five even though our menus are developed for one and two year-olds also. We did this so meal planning would not be too complicated when cooking for preschoolers of different ages. Children under the age of three will be served amounts slightly above the CACFP requirements. However, it has been our experience that children this age have no problem consuming this larger portion. Children three through five may want second servings, but the recipes do not allow for seconds in this age group. You may need to prepare more than the minimum, depending on appetites and budget.

You may be able to use one or more of the serving amounts (6, 20, 50, or 100) we have used in the recipes to plan your meals. For example, if you have 85 children and teachers, you might cook for 100 to allow for seconds. If you have 110 children and teachers, you might cook the amounts for 100 and for 20. You can determine quantities for numbers of servings other than those we have provided by using the factor method illustrated on page 181.

The recipes include a variety of foods that are moderate in saturated fat, cholesterol, salt, and sugar. Food items and cooking techniques are designed to increase the iron intake of children and the menus include an abundance of fruit, vegetables, and whole grains.

All of our menus include a Vitamin A vegetable or fruit at least twice a week, a Vitamin C vegetable or fruit daily, and several iron-rich foods each day. (See CACFP recommendations on pp. 18, 20.) In some of the menus we have specified a particular kind of juice or fruit to ensure that children receive a good source of Vitamin C each day. Where Vitamin C was provided by some other food, we left the choice of the juice or fruit to the meal planner.

On Monday mornings, we have added an optional protein food item to supplement the children's weekend diet. We were concerned that some children may not be receiving their recommended daily allowances (CRDAs) of some nutrients, espcially protein, during the weekend. For this same reason, Friday afternoon snacks have a required component that is a protein source and an optional third food component.

A special note about milk fat: the American Academy of Pediatrics and the American Heart Association recommend lowering the amount of saturated fat in diets for children over two years of age. Neither committee recommends restricting fat in the diets of children under two, however. You should consider using skim milk for children over two and whole milk for children under two. Some pediatricians recommend using two percent milk as a compromise for families and child care settings that include children over and under two.

We recommend that parents consult their pediatrician if they have specific concerns about the diet of their child.

Note that cooking times may vary on recipes depending on the oven and the size of the pan(s). Be sure to check your oven frequently when you prepare a recipe for the first time. You might want to make a note in your cookbook about how long you needed to cook the food item.

The shorthand we use for measurements in the recipes is:
- c = cup(s);
- T = tablespoon(s);
- t = teaspoon(s)
- lb = pound(s);
- oz = ounce(s);
- #10 can = number 10 can(s);
- gal = gallon(s); qt = quart(s);
- Please note the carrot sign (🥕) indicates a special, time-saving shortcut we have provided you:

> 🥕 = use Quick Reference Chart (inside front cover, last page and inside back cover) to estimate purchase amount.

CHAPTER FIVE

MENUS AND RECIPES: WEEK ONE

WEEK ONE

Monday morning's menu includes a recipe for Egg Puff, a baked version of scrambled eggs; it is a great way to start the week.

Tuesday's stir-fried broccoli recipe shows a different way to prepare this delicious vegetable. It takes a little extra time to stir-fry, so be sure to plan ahead.

On Wednesday you introduce mashed sweet potatoes. The children may be curious about the color.

Thursday's Apple Gelatin should be made a day ahead of time to give it a chance to gel.

Friday's afternoon snack includes Peanut Butter Balls. This can be incorporated into a classroom cooking activity. Children enjoy preparing this recipe.

WEEKLY MENU RECORD

Provider's Name _Alice_

	DAY/DATE	MON 10/1	TUE 10/2	WED 10/3	THU 10/4	FRI 10/5
BREAKFAST	Fluid Milk	MILK	MILK	MILK	MILK	MILK
	Juice or Fruit or Vegetable	MAN ORANGES	APPLE JUICE	APPLE SAUCE	GRAPES	BANANA
	Bread or Cereal or Alternate	TOAST	CEREAL	FR TOAST STICKS	WW BAGEL	CINNAMON RAISIN WHEEL
	Additional Foods (optional)	EGG PUFF				
LUNCH/SUPPER	Fluid Milk	MILK	MILK	MILK	MILK	MILK
	Main Dish					PIMENTO CHEESE SAND
	Meat or Alternate	CHILI	TURKEY BURGER PIE	MEATBALLS/GRAVY	SALMON CAKES	PC SANDWICH
	Juice or Fruit or Vegetable	BAKED APPLE	PEARS/BROCCOLI	FR COLESLAW SW POTATO	CORN/ APPLE GELATIN	PEACHES
	Bread or Alternate	CORN BREAD	WHOLE GRAIN BREAD	BREAD	BISCUIT	PC SANDWICH
SNACK	Fluid Milk	GRAHAM CRACKERS APPLE JUICE	BANANA BREAD OJ	SODA CRACKERS CHEDDAR CHEESE APPLE JUICE	ANIMAL CRACKERS TOMATO JUICE	P.B. BALLS APPLES MILK
	Meat or Alternate					
	Juice or Fruit or Vegetable					
	Bread or Cereal or Alternate					

50 CHILD CARE COOKBOOK

MONDAY

MENU ITEM	SERVING SIZE=REQUIREMENT
	BREAKFAST
Toast, thin-slice bread	1 slice = 1 bread
Mandarin Oranges	$\frac{1}{2}$ c = 1 fruit
Milk, fluid	$\frac{3}{4}$ c = 1 milk
Egg Puff	1 egg puff = $\frac{1}{2}$ meat (optional)
	LUNCH/SUPPER
Chili	$\frac{3}{4}$ c = 1 meat; $\frac{1}{2}$ fruit/vegetable
Baked Apples	$\frac{1}{4}$ c (or $\frac{1}{2}$ whole apple) = $\frac{1}{2}$ fruit/vegetable
Corn Bread	1 serving = 1 bread
Milk, fluid	$\frac{3}{4}$ c = 1 milk
	SNACK
Graham Crackers (5" x 2$\frac{1}{2}$")	1$\frac{1}{2}$ crackers = 1 bread
Juice, 100% fruit	$\frac{1}{2}$ c = 1 fruit

Note: Refer to the Quick Reference Chart (inside front cover, last page, and inside back cover) for purchasing quantities of canned mandarin oranges. When in season, fresh oranges may be cheaper.

One serving of chili contains meat ($\frac{1}{2}$) and beans ($\frac{1}{2}$) to equal one full meat requirement.

CHILD CARE COOKBOOK 51

EGG PUFF

1 egg puff = $^1/_2$ meat (optional)
BAKE: 20 MINUTES AT 350°

	6	20	50	100
Eggs, medium	2	6	16	32
Biscuit Mix, enriched (p. 142)	$^1/_4$ c	$^3/_4$ c	2 c	$3^3/_4$ c
Cheddar Cheese	2 oz	7 oz	$1^3/_4$ lb	2 lb+2 oz
Milk	5 oz	2 c+2 oz	$5^1/_2$ c	2 qt+3 c
Dry Mustard	$^1/_4$ t	1 t	$2^1/_2$ t	$1^1/_2$ T
Cooking Spray				

1. Grease muffin pans (one muffin container per child) with cooking spray.
2. Grate cheese.
3. Mix all ingredients with hand mixer.
4. Pour $^1/_4$ cup of mixture into each muffin container.
5. Bake about 20 minutes at 350 degrees. Centers should be firm.
6. Let sit for 5 minutes before serving.

Note: Egg puff can be served on a toasted junior size hamburger bun, English muffin or biscuit to resemble a fast food-type egg sandwich. You could substitute the bun, muffin or biscuit for the toast in this menu.

CHILI

$3/4$ c = 1 meat; $1/2$ fruit/vegetable

	6	20	50	100
Ground Beef	$1/2$ lb	$1\frac{1}{2}$ lb	$3\frac{1}{2}$ lb	7 lb
Light Kidney Beans	1–16 oz can	$2\frac{1}{2}$ –16 oz cans	1–#10 can	2 –#10 cans
Tomatoes, canned	1–16 oz can	2 –28 oz cans	1–#10 can + 1–16 oz can	2 –#10 + 2 –16 oz cans
Chili Powder	1 t	1 T	$1/4$ c	$1/2$ c
Spice Mix (p. 142)	1 T	$2\frac{1}{2}$ T	$1/2$ c	$3/4$ c
Garlic Powder	1 t	1 T	$1/4$ c	$1/2$ c
Onion Powder	1 t	1 T	$1/4$ c	$1/2$ c

1. Brown ground beef in iron skillet and drain fat.
2. Chop tomatoes in a blender.
3. Put meat and all remaining ingredients into a large pot.
4. Heat to boiling.
5. Turn down heat. Simmer for 2 hours — longer, if possible.

MONDAY MONDAY MONDAY MONDAY MONDAY MONDAY MONDAY

BAKED APPLES

$^1/_4$ c (or $^1/_2$ whole apple) = $^1/_2$ fruit/vegetable

Bake: 45 minutes at 350°

	6	20	50
Margarine	1$^1/_2$ T	4 T	8 T
Sliced Apples, canned	2–20 oz cans	1–#10 can	2–#10 cans
Sugar	$^1/_4$ c	$^1/_2$ c	1 c
Cinnamon	1 t	1 T	2 T

1. Use pan(s) with 1" sides. Grease pan(s) with margarine.
2. Put apples and liquid in pans.
3. Sprinkle with sugar and cinnamon. (Omit sugar if canned apples are packed with sugar or corn syrup.)
4. Bake for 45 minutes at 350 degrees.
5. If preparing for 100, make 2 batches at 50.

Note: You might want to substitute fresh apples, especially if you are cooking a smaller quantity. Refer to the following chart and directions if you are using fresh apples.

	6	20	50	100
Fresh apples, small	3	10	25	50
Water	$^1/_4$ c	$^2/_3$ c	1$^1/_3$ c	2$^1/_2$ c

1. Wash and slice apples $^1/_4$" thick, removing core and seeds.
2. Follow above procedure. Add water before placing apples into pan.

CORNBREAD

1 Serving = 1 bread

Bake: 15-20 minutes at 425°

	6	20	50	100
Yellow Corn Meal	³/₄ c	1¹/₂ c	2¹/₂ c	5 c
Flour, enriched or whole grain	³/₄ c	1¹/₂ c	2¹/₂ c	5 c
Baking Powder	1 T	2 T	4 T	8 T
Milk	³/₄ c	1¹/₂ c	3 c	6 c
Eggs, medium	1	2	4	8
Margarine	¹/₄ c	¹/₂ c	1 c	1¹/₂ c

1. Combine dry ingredients.
2. Add milk, eggs, and margarine.
3. Beat until smooth — about 1 minute.
4. Lightly grease cast iron skillet with shortening.
5. Preheat skillet in oven at 425 degrees for 15 minutes.
6. Pour batter into preheated skillet and bake at 425 degrees for 15-20 minutes.
7. Cut into portions equal to number of children to be served, at least ½ ounce serving per child.

TUESDAY

MENU ITEM   **SERVING SIZE=REQUIREMENT**

BREAKFAST

Cereal, dry	$^1/_3$ c = 1 bread
Milk, fluid	$^3/_4$ c = 1 milk
Orange Juice	$^1/_2$ c = 1 fruit

LUNCH/SUPPER

Turkeyburger Pie	1 serving = 1 meat
Stir-fried Broccoli	$^1/_4$ c = $^1/_2$ fruit/vegetable
Pears, canned	$^1/_4$ c ($^1/_2$ pear with juice) = $^1/_2$ fruit/vegetable
Bread, whole-grain, regular slice	$^1/_2$ slice = 1 bread
Milk, fluid	$^3/_4$ c = 1 milk

SNACK

Banana Bread	1 muffin = 1 bread
Juice, 100% fruit	$^1/_2$ c = 1 fruit

Note: One serving of Turkeyburger Pie contains turkey ($^1/_2$), cheese, and eggs ($^1/_2$) to equal one meat requirement.

TURKEYBURGER PIE

1 serving = 1 meat
Bake: 30-40 minutes at 400°

	6	20	50	100
Ground Turkey	1 lb	1 lb 7 oz	3 lb 8 oz	7 lb
Large Onion, chopped, or	$1/4$ c	$1/2$ c	$1^1/2$ c	3 c
Dry Minced Onion	1 T	$1/4$ c	$2/3$ c	$1^1/3$ c
Mozzarella Cheese	2 oz	$1/2$ lb	$1^1/3$ lb	2 lb 5 oz
Cheddar Cheese	2 oz	$1/2$ lb	$1^1/3$ lb	2 lb 5 oz
Egg Whites, medium	1	3	6	12
Whole Eggs, medium	2	4	6	12
Milk	$1^1/2$ c	$2^1/2$ c	$6^1/2$ c	3 qt+1 c
Spice Mix (p. 142)	$1/2$ t	1 t	$1/4$ c	$1/2$ c
Biscuit Mix (p. 142)	$3/4$ c	$1^1/3$ c	$3^1/2$ c	7 c

1. Brown ground turkey in an iron skillet and drain.
2. Spread meat on bottom of pan(s) sprayed with cooking spray.
3. Chop onion in food processor and sprinkle over meat.
4. Grate or shred cheese.
5. Divide cheese evenly among the pans and sprinkle over meat and onion.
6. Separate eggs as indicated above and discard the yolk(s).
7. In a very large bowl, combine eggs, milk, spice mix, and biscuit mix. Mix thoroughly.
8. Pour mixture over meat and cheese.
9. Bake at 400 degrees for 30-40 minutes or until brown and firm.
10. Allow to stand for 10 minutes before cutting into servings.
11. Cut into portions equal to number of children to be served.

STIR-FRIED BROCCOLI

$1/4$ c = $1/2$ fruit/vegetable

	6	20	50	100
Broccoli, fresh	$3/4$ lb	2 lb 1 oz	5 lb 3 oz	10 lb 5 oz
Oil	1 T	$1/4$ c	$1/2$ c	1 c
Garlic Clove(s)	1	2	3	6
Ground Ginger	$1/4$ t	$3/4$ t	$1^1/_2$ T	3 T
Chicken Broth	$1/4$ c	$3/4$ c	$1^1/_2$ c	3 c
Soy Sauce	2 T	$1/4$ c	$2/3$ c	$3/4$ c
Sesame Seeds (optional)				

1. Cut fresh broccoli into bite-size pieces, including the inner stems. Also, broccoli leaves are rich in iron and may be used in moderation.
2. Heat oil in large iron skillet or wok over medium high heat.
3. Add garlic cloves and ginger and saute until brown. Remove cloves from oil with slotted spoon.
4. Put broccoli in skillet or wok.
5. Cook, stirring constantly, for 10 minutes. Halfway through cooking time, add chicken broth.
6. Add soy sauce. Stir-fry for 5 minutes longer.
7. Remove broccoli from pan with slotted spoon and place on serving dish. Reuse skillet to stir-fry remaining broccoli.
8. Repeat steps 2-7 with remaining batches of broccoli.
9. Keep warm in 200 degree oven until ready to serve.
10. Sprinkle with sesame seeds, if desired.

Note: This recipe may seem a bit complicated for broccoli, but ginger and soy sauce give it a different flavor that children seem to like. Lunch on this day should allow you enough time to make this recipe.

Divide all ingredients into 2 or 3 batches if cooking for a large group.

BANANA BREAD

1 muffin = 1 bread
Bake: 45 minutes at 350°

	20	50	100
Biscuit Mix (p. 142)	4 c	10 c	20 c
Sugar	1 c	2¹/₂ c	5 c
Eggs, medium	3	7	14
Milk	²/₃ c	1²/₃ c	3¹/₃ c
Bananas, mashed	1¹/₂ c	3³/₄ c	7¹/₂ c

1. Mix all ingredients with mixer on medium speed.
2. Spray muffin tins with cooking spray.
3. Pour muffin mix into greased tins.
4. Bake at 350 degrees for 45 minutes.

Note: If serving fewer than 20, refrigerate or freeze unused muffins to serve at a later date. See page (p. 44) for information about storing leftovers.

TUESDAY TUESDAY TUESDAY TUESDAY TUESDAY TUESDAY TUESDAY TUESDAY

WEDNESDAY

MENU ITEM	SERVING SIZE=REQUIREMENT

BREAKFAST

French Toast Sticks	3 sticks = 1 bread
Applesauce ⬦	$\frac{1}{2}$ c = 1 fruit
Milk, fluid ⬦	$\frac{3}{4}$ c = 1 milk

LUNCH/SUPPER

Meatballs and Gravy	2 meatballs = 1 meat
Sweet Potatoes	$\frac{1}{4}$ c = 1 fruit/vegetable
Fruit Cocktail ⬦	$\frac{1}{4}$ c = 1 fruit/vegetable
Bread, regular slice ⬦	$\frac{1}{2}$ slice = 1 bread
Milk, fluid ⬦	$\frac{3}{4}$ c = 1 milk

SNACK

Cheddar Cheese ⬦	$\frac{1}{4}$ oz = $\frac{1}{2}$ meat
Crackers, soda ⬦	4 squares = $\frac{1}{2}$ bread
Orange Juice, 100% fruit ⬦	$\frac{1}{2}$ c = 1 fruit

PLAN AHEAD TIP: Make Pimento Cheese mixture for Friday Lunch/Supper. Make Apple Gelatin for Thursday.

FRENCH TOAST STICKS

3 sticks = 1 bread

	6	20	50	100
Egg Whites, medium	1	2	6	12
Whole Eggs, medium	1	3	6	12
Milk	1/3 c	1 1/4 c	3 c	6 1/4 c
Cinnamon	1/2 t	1 t	1 T	2 T
Bread, thin sliced	6	20	50	100
Margarine				

1. Separate eggs as indicated above and discard the yolk(s).
2. Mix eggs, milk, and cinnamon in a blender or with a wire whip until thoroughly blended.
3. Heat iron griddle over medium heat.
4. Melt 1 tablespoon margarine and coat griddle. Be sure to coat griddle with margarine each time you cook another batch of French Toast Sticks.
5. Dip bread in egg mixture and place on hot griddle.
6. Brown bread on both sides.
7. Remove from griddle and cut each bread slice into three strips.
8. Store on cookie sheet in warm oven until time to serve.

Note: Instead of serving syrup with French Toast Sticks, let the children dip them into their applesauce. If you have time, put applesauce in a large pan and add vanilla extract (1/2 t = 6 servings, 1 T = 20, 2 1/2 T = 50, 1/2 c = 100). Sprinkle with cinnamon and dot with margarine. Warm applesauce while heating French Toast Sticks. Great on a cold day!

To freeze French Toast for later use:
1. Remove bread from griddle and stack on aluminum foil. Wrap, date, and freeze.
2. When time to serve, remove French Toast from freezer and let thaw 30 minutes, if possible.
3. Preheat oven to 350 degrees.
4. Cut each slightly-thawed piece of French Toast into three strips and place on an ungreased cookie sheet.
5. Cook for 15 minutes or until heated through.

MEATBALLS

2 meatballs = 1 meat
Bake: 20-30 minutes at 350°

	6	20	50	100
Ground Turkey	1 lb	2 lb 12 oz	$6^1/_2$ lb	13 lb
Tomato Sauce	$^1/_3$ c	$^3/_4$ c	2 c	4 c
Rolled Oats	$^1/_2$ c	1 c	2 c	4 c
Eggs, medium	1	2	6	11
Onion Powder	1 t	2 t	$1^1/_2$ T	$^1/_4$ c

1. Mix all ingredients together.
2. Use $^1/_4$ cup or #16 scoop to measure total serving size of meat. Divide that quantity of meat in half to make two meatballs per child.
3. Place meatballs on at least a one inch-deep pan sprayed with cooking spray.
4. Bake at 350 degrees for 20-30 minutes, until brown.
5. Drain off fat and serve with gravy.

Note: For ease in shaping meatballs, wet hands slightly. For larger portions, you can press meat into pan coated with cooking spray. After baking, cut into equal serving sizes. Increase cooking time to 45-50 minutes.

GRAVY

	6	20	50	100
Chicken Bouillon	1 cube	3 cubes	$^5/_8$ c granules	$1^1/_4$ c granules
Boiling Water	1 c	3 c	7 c	14 c
Margarine	1 T	$^1/_4$ c	$1^1/_4$ sticks	$2^1/_2$ sticks
Flour	1 to 2 T	3 to 4 T	$^1/_2$ to $^2/_3$ c	1 to $1^1/_3$ c

1. Dissolve bouillon cubes in boiling water.
2. Melt margarine in sauce pan. When margarine is bubbly, add flour gradually. Stir constantly and add a little hot bouillon while stirring.
3. Pour remaining mixture into bouillon, stirring constantly to avoid lumps. Cook until thick.

SWEET POTATOES

$^1/_4$ c = 1 fruit/vegetable

	6	20	50	100
Sweet Potatoes, fresh	1$^1/_4$ lb	3$^3/_4$ lb	9$^1/_4$ lb	18$^1/_4$ lb
Water	1$^1/_4$ c	1 qt	2$^1/_2$ qt	1 gal+1 qt
Milk	3 oz	$^3/_4$ c	1$^3/_4$ c	3$^1/_2$ c
Margarine, softened	1 T	$^1/_4$ c	$^1/_2$ c	1 c

1. Wash, peel, and cut potatoes into quarters or medium-size chunks.
2. Boil potatoes until tender, about 25 minutes. Drain.
3. Mash potatoes in mixer on low speed until smooth.
4. Warm milk in saucepan over medium heat. Gradually add just enough milk to potatoes to moisten.
5. Add margarine while beating on low speed.
6. Mix on high speed until blended and potatoes are light and fluffy.
7. Serve with #16 scoop ($^1/_4$ c).

Note: Children may not be used to "orange" mashed potatoes, but try this recipe several times. Make it an adventure by "growing" a sweet potato in the classroom. Remember to be positive.

THURSDAY

MENU ITEM	SERVING SIZE=REQUIREMENT

BREAKFAST

Bagels, whole wheat ⛟   ½ bagel = 1 bread

Grapes, sliced in quarters ⛟   ½ c = 1 fruit

Milk, fluid ⛟   ¾ c = 1 milk

LUNCH/SUPPER

Salmon Cakes   1 cake = 1 meat

Corn ⛟   ¼ c = ½ fruit/vegetable

Apple Gelatin   ¼ c = ½ fruit/vegetable

Biscuit   1 biscuit = 1 bread

Milk, fluid ⛟   ¾ c = 1 milk

SNACK

Animal Crackers ⛟   7 crackers = 1 bread

Juice, 100% fruit ⛟   ½ c = 1 fruit

Note: One serving of Salmon Cakes contains salmon (¾) and eggs (¼) to equal one meat requirement.

PLAN AHEAD TIP: Soak raisins for Friday morning Cinnamon Raisin Wheels. You can make Peanut Butter Balls today for Friday's snack.

SALMON CAKES

1 cake = 1 meat
Bake: 45 minutes at 350°

	6	20	50	100
Salmon, canned	1–15 oz. can	3–15 oz cans	1–64 oz + 2–15 oz cans	3–64 oz cans
Buttermilk	2 T	¼ c	½ c	1 c
Eggs, medium	1	3	6	12
Lemon Juice	½ t	1 t	1 T	2 T
Chopped Onions	1 T	¼ c	⅔ c	1⅓ c
Bread Crumbs	¼ c	¾ c	2 c	4 c
Flour	2 t	1½ T	¼ c	½ c
Oil				

1. Drain salmon.
2. Mix all ingredients together and make into patties using ¼ cup measure or #16 scoop.
3. Lightly oil shallow baking pans and brush tops of patties with oil.
4. Bake at 350 degrees for 45 minutes or until brown.
5. Serve Salmon Cakes with ketchup; children enjoy dipping.

Note: If you do not normally stock buttermilk, you can use regular milk. However, buttermilk does keep in the refrigerator a long time and can also be used in the biscuit recipe for today's menu.

APPLE GELATIN

$^1/_4$ c = $^1/_2$ fruit/vegetable

	6	20	50	100
Gelatin	1 heaping T	3 T	7 T	13 T
Apple Juice,				
100% fruit juice	2 c	6 c	3 qt + $^1/_2$ c	1$^1/_2$ gal + 1 c
Sugar	2 t	2 T	$^1/_4$ c	$^1/_2$ c

1. Dissolve gelatin in juice. Stir until dissolved.
2. Boil gelatin mixture and stir.
3. If you have any extra fruit (pears, peaches, fruit cocktail), you could add it to the gelatin mixture at this point.
4. Pour into mold or pan and refrigerate until gelled, about 3 hours.

BISCUIT

1 biscuit = 1 bread
Bake: 12-15 minutes at 400°

	20	50	100
Flour, enriched	$1^1/_3$ c	3 c+3 oz	$6^3/_4$ c
Baking Powder	2 t	1 T + 2 t	3 T + 1 t
Salt	$^1/_4$ t	$^3/_4$ t	$1^3/_4$ t
Vegetable Oil	$^1/_4$ c	$^1/_2$ c + 1 T	$1^1/_4$ c
Milk or Buttermilk	$^3/_4$ c	$1^1/_2$ c + 1 T	$3^1/_3$ c
Cooking Spray			

1. Combine dry ingredients.
2. Add oil and milk. Stir until a soft dough is formed.
3. Turn onto a floured board and knead 5 times.
4. Roll out to $^1/_2$ inch thickness.
5. Cut with 2 inch biscuit cutter.
6. Place biscuits on cookie sheet (sprayed with cooking spray) with sides touching.
7. Bake at 400 degrees for 12-15 minutes or until lightly browned.

Note: If serving fewer than 20, refrigerate or freeze unused biscuits to serve at a later date. See p. 44, for information about accounting for leftovers and frozen items on your production plan.

FRIDAY

MENU ITEM

BREAKFAST

Cinnamon Raisin Wheels   1 wheel = 1 bread

Bananas ⩗ $1/2$ c = 1 fruit

Milk, fluid ⩗ $3/4$ c = 1 milk

LUNCH/SUPPER

Pimento Cheese Sandwiches   1 sandwich = 1 meat; 1 bread

Cream of Tomato Soup $1/2$ c = $1/2$ fruit/vegetable

Peaches ⩗ $1/4$ c = $1/2$ fruit/vegetable

Milk, fluid ⩗ $3/4$ c = 1 milk

SNACK

Peanut Butter Balls   4 balls = 1 meat

Milk, fluid ⩗ $3/4$ c = 1 milk

Sliced Apples ⩗ $1/4$ c or $1/2$ apple = $1/2$ fruit (optional)

CINNAMON RAISIN WHEELS

1 serving = 1 meat
Bake: 30-40 minutes at 400°

	20	50
Raisins	½ c	1¼ c
Water	½ c	1¼ c
Yogurt, plain	⅔ c	1⅔ c
Yeast	1 pack (1 T)	3 packs (3 T)
Margarine	2 T	5 T
Eggs	1	3
Biscuit Mix (p. 142)	4 c	10 c
Cinnamon	1 t	1 T
Sugar	¼ c	⅔ c
Cooking Spray		

1. Soak raisins overnight in water. Drain and save liquid.
2. Heat raisin water to 115 degrees, adding tap water to equal required amount. Use a candy thermometer to measure temperature.
3. Dissolve yeast in warmed raisin water and let sit for 10 minutes.
4. Stir in yogurt, margarine, raisins, egg, and ½ of biscuit mix.
5. Mix at low speed for 2 minutes, scraping sides of bowl.
6. Stir in remaining biscuit mix, add more biscuit mix if necessary to form a stiff dough. (For easier handling when making for 50, separate dough into two equal parts.)

(continued on next page)

7. Roll dough on a floured surface forming a long rectangle.
8. Mix cinnamon and sugar together and sprinkle over dough. Cut each rectangle in half.
9. Roll each rectangle tightly to form a long cylinder.
10. With a floured knife, slice each cylinder into equal slices, about 1 inch thick.
11. Place on a cookie sheet coated with cooking spray, cut side down. Cover with a clean cloth and put in warm, dry place to rise for 30 minutes.
12. Bake 15-20 minutes at 375 degrees, or until brown.

Note: If serving fewer than 20, refrigerate or freeze unused wheels to serve at a later date. See p. 44, for Production Plan information on leftovers and frozen items. For 100, make 2 batches of 50.

PIMENTO CHEESE SANDWICHES

1 sandwich = 1 meat; 1 bread

	6	20	50	100
Cheddar Cheese	9 oz	2 lb	4¾ lb	9½ lb
Mayonnaise	¼ c	½ c	1½ c	3 c
Worcestershire Sauce	¼ t	1 t	½ T	1 T
Pimentos, chopped	½ of whole	1 whole	2 whole	4 whole
Bread, thin-sliced	12	40	100	200

1. Grate cheese.
2. Mix cheese, mayonnaise, and Worcestershire sauce with a spoon in large bowl. Do not use a blender or mixer.
3. Add chopped pimento.
4. Mix thoroughly and refrigerate for several hours or overnight.
5. Put ¼ cup or #16 scoop of pimento cheese mixture on each sandwich.

Note: This mixture tastes best if made one or two days in advance.

CREAM OF TOMATO SOUP

½ cup = ½ fruit/vegetable

	6	20	50	100
Tomatoes, canned	8 oz	20 oz	2½–#2 cans	1–#10 can
Tomato Sauce, canned	16 oz	40 oz	1–#10 can	2–#10 cans
Onion, finely chopped	2 T	⅓ c	¾ c	1½ c
Bay Leaf	½	½	1	2
Baking Soda	¼ t	1 t	1½ t	1 T
Margarine	1 T	2½ T	5 T	10 T
Flour, enriched or whole-grain	2½ T	½ c	⅔ c	¾ c
Salt	¾ t	2 t	1½ T	3 T
Pepper	dash	dash	½ t	1 t
Sugar	1 T	¼ c	½ c	1 c
Milk	1½ c	3½ c	½ gal	1 gal

1. Chop tomatoes in blender.
2. Combine tomatoes, tomato sauce, onion, and bay leaf in large pot. Bring mixture to a boil.
3. Reduce heat to simmer and add baking soda.
4. While tomato mixture simmers, melt margarine in a separate sauce pan. Reduce heat.
5. Add flour to melted margarine. Stir in salt, pepper, and sugar until well blended into a paste.
6. Gradually add milk to margarine and flour mixture, stirring constantly with a wire whip to avoid lumps. Keep warm over low heat.
7. Ten minutes before serving, add milk mixture to tomato base. Stir well and heat through.

PEANUT BUTTER BALLS

4 balls = 1 meat

	20	50	100
Bran Flake Cereal	1 c	2 c	5 c
Dried Apricots	⅓ c	¾ c	1½ c
Dry Milk	6 T	1 c	2 c
Peanut Butter	1¼ c	3 c	6¼ c
Honey	⅓ c	¾ c	1½ c

1. Crush half of cereal in food processor and set aside.
2. Chop apricots in food processor.
3. Add dry milk, honey, remainder of cereal, and peanut butter to apricots in food processor.
4. Pulse food processor on and off, scraping sides until mixture is blended.
5. Using your hands, roll reanut butter mixture into small, bite-size balls.
6. Coat balls with crushed cereal.
7. Store in refrigerator or freezer.

Note: If serving fewer than 20, refrigerate or freeze unused Peanut Butter Balls to serve at a later date. See p. 44 for information about leftovers and frozen items.

CHAPTER SIX

MENUS AND RECIPES: WEEK TWO

WEEK TWO MENUS

Monday's lunch menu is a well-balanced vegetarian meal.

Tuesday's Applesauce Hermits taste great when spread with apple butter.

Wednesday's lunch menu is all finger food. No silverware to wash today!

Thursday's afternoon snack suggests you serve apple juice with added Vitamin C to help meet the daily minimum requirement of this vitamin.

Friday's Carrot and Raisin Salad tastes best when made a day ahead of time.

WEEKLY MENU RECORD

Provider's Name _Alice_

	DAY/DATE	MON 10/8	TUE 10/9	WED 10/10	THU 10/11	FRI 10/12
BREAKFAST	Fluid Milk	MILK	MILK	MILK	MILK	MILK
	Juice or Fruit or Vegetable	ORANGES	PINEAPPLE/BANANA	TOMATO JUICE	APPLESAUCE	GRAPES
	Bread or Cereal or Alternate	ENG MUFFIN	APPLESAUCE HER	CEREAL	CINNAMON TOAST	CEREAL
	Additional Foods (optional)	SAUSAGE BALLS				
LUNCH/SUPPER	Fluid Milk	MILK	MILK	MILK	MILK	MILK
	Main Dish	CHEESE PIZZA	MAC BEEF & CHEESE	HAM & CHEESE SAND	CHICKEN SPAGHETTI	HAMBURGER/ROLL
	Meat or Alternate	CHS PZ/COT CHEESE	MAC BEEF	HAM & CHEESE SAND	CHICKEN SPAGHETTI	HAMBURGER/ROLL
	Juice or Fruit or Vegetable	PINEAPPLE TOSSED SALAD/PIZZA	FR COCKTAIL	RAW VEGGIES	FINGER GELATIN PEAS & CARROTS FR COCKTAIL	CARROT/RAISIN SALAD
	Bread or Alternate	PIZZA	MAC BEEF	HAM & CHEESE SAND	CHICKEN SPAGHETTI	HAMBURGER/ROLL
SNACK	Fluid Milk	GRAHAM CRACKER MILK	BREADSTICKS JUICE	PUMPKIN COOKIES MILK	BRAN MUFFINS APPLE JUICE	ANIMAL CRACKERS YOGURT JUICE
	Meat or Alternate					
	Juice or Fruit or Vegetable					
	Bread or Cereal or Alternate					

MONDAY

MENU ITEM

SERVING SIZE=REQUIREMENT

BREAKFAST

English Muffin ☗   ½ muffin = ½ bread

Oranges (or fresh fruit in season) ☗   ½ orange = ½ fruit

Milk, fluid ☗   ¾ c = 1 milk

Sausage Balls   3 balls = ½ meat (optional)

LUNCH/SUPPER

Cheese Pizza   1 serving = 1 bread, ¼ fruit/vegetable, ½ meat

Tossed Salad   ¼ c = ½ fruit/vegetable

Cottage Cheese and Pineapple   ¼ c = ¼ fruit/vegetable, ½ meat

Milk, fluid ☗   ¾ c = 1 milk

SNACK

Graham Crackers ☗   3 crackers = 1 bread

Milk, fluid ☗   ½ c = 1 milk

SAUSAGE BALLS

3 balls = $\frac{1}{2}$ meat (optional)

Bake: 15 minutes at 350°

	6	20	50	100
Turkey Sausage	$\frac{1}{4}$ lb	1 lb	2 lb 2 oz	4 lb 4 oz
Mozzarella Cheese	3 oz	$\frac{1}{2}$ lb	$1\frac{1}{4}$ lb	$2\frac{1}{2}$ lb
Ground Red Pepper	$\frac{1}{8}$ t	$\frac{1}{2}$ t	2 t	4 t
Soy Sauce	$\frac{1}{2}$ t	$\frac{1}{2}$ T	4 t	2 T+2 t
Biscuit Mix (p. 142)	$\frac{1}{2}$ c	$1\frac{1}{2}$ c + 3 T	4 c + 2 T	$8\frac{1}{4}$ c
Milk	3 T	$\frac{1}{2}$ c + 1 T	$1\frac{1}{4}$ c + 2 T	$2\frac{3}{4}$ c
Cooking Spray				

1. Brown the sausage, drain off fat, and crumble sausage.
2. Shred cheese.
3. Mix cheese and remaining ingredients together well, forming a soft dough. (Red pepper adds an interesting, spicy flavor to this recipe without being "hot.")
4. Add crumbled sausage and mix well.
5. Using wet hands, form mixture into one-inch balls and place on pans greased with cooking spray.
6. Bake at 350 degrees for 15 minutes.

Note: Cooked Sausage Balls freeze well. To serve, let balls thaw and then warm in 350 degree oven for 5 minutes. If frozen, warm for 20 minutes at 350 degrees.

CHEESE PIZZA

1 SERVING = 1 bread, 1/4 fruit/vegetable, 1/2 meat
Bake: 20 minutes at 400°

	20	50	100
Yeast	1 1/2 T	4 T	1/2 c
Flour, enriched or whole-grain	3 1/3 c	8 c	16 c
Water	2 T	1/3 c	2/3 c
Milk	2/3 c	1 1/2 c	3 c
Oil	6 T	1 c	2 c
Honey	3 T	1/2 c	1 c
Tomato Sauce	2 1/2 c	#3 can	#10 can
Spice Mix (p. 142)	(1 T per pizza)		
Mozzarella Cheese	1 lb 8 oz	3 lb 12 oz	7 lb 8 oz
Parmesan Cheese, grated	2/3 c	1 1/4 c	2 1/2 c

1. Mix yeast with half the flour and set aside.
2. Heat milk, water, oil, and honey to 115 degrees. Use candy thermometer to measure temperature.
3. Pour milk mixture into flour and yeast. Mix, then knead for three minutes.
4. Add remaining flour and mix with dough hook or by hand.
5. Allow dough to sit covered for 10 minutes.
6. Divide dough into number of pizzas to be made (20=2 or 3 parts, 50=5 parts, 100=10 parts).
7. Roll each out on a floured board.
8. Place rolled dough in pizza pans and, using oiled fingers, spread dough to rim forming slightly raised edges.
9. Spread tomato sauce on dough and sprinkle with spice mix.
10. Shred mozzarella cheese.
11. Cover pizza(s) with shredded mozzarella and sprinkle Parmesan cheese over the top.
12. Bake for 20 minutes at 400 degrees.

Note: If serving fewer than 20, refrigerate or freeze unused pizzas to serve at a later date. See p. 44 for information about leftovers and frozen items.

PLAN AHEAD TIP: Double the pizza dough recipe and refrigerate unused portion. Use it to make bread sticks for Tuesday's snack.

TOSSED SALAD

$^1/_4$ c $= {}^1/_2$ fruit/vegetable

	6	20	50	100
Lettuce, shredded	$1^1/_2$ c	5 c	2 lb	4 lb
Tomatoes, whole	$^1/_4$	1	2	4
Cucumbers, whole	$^1/_4$	$^1/_2$	$1^1/_2$	3
Salad Dressing, low-fat				

1. Rinse vegetables.
2. Chop in small pieces.
3. Toss together.
4. Serve with any of the low-fat salad dressings currently available.

Note: Serve the dressing on the side; children like to use it as "dip."

COTTAGE CHEESE AND PINEAPPLE

$^1/_4$ c $= {}^1/_4$ fruit/vegetable, $^1/_2$ meat

	6	20	50	100
Crushed Pineapple, canned	$^3/_4$ c	$2^1/_2$ c	2–#$2^1/_2$ cans	1–#10 can
Cottage Cheese, low-fat	$^3/_4$ c	$2^1/_2$ c	$6^1/_4$ c	$12^1/_2$ c

1. Drain pineapple.
2. Combine pineapple with cottage cheese.

TUESDAY

MENU ITEM	SERVING SIZE=REQUIREMENT

BREAKFAST

Applesauce Hermits	1 biscuit = 1 bread
Pineapple and Bananas	½ c = 1 fruit
Milk, fluid	¾ c = 1 milk

LUNCH/SUPPER

Macaroni Beef and Cheese	1 serving = 1 meat; 1 bread
Steamed Broccoli	¼ c = ½ fruit/vegetable
Fruit Cocktail	¼ c = ½ fruit/vegetable
Milk, fluid	¾ c = 1 milk

SNACK

| Breadsticks | 1 breadstick = 1 bread |
| Juice, 100% fruit | ½ c = 1 fruit |

Note: One serving of Macaroni Beef and Cheese includes one meat requirement consisting of ½ meat and ½ cheese, and one bread requirement.

PLAN AHEAD TIP: Make Finger Gelatin for Wednesday's Lunch/Supper.

APPLESAUCE HERMITS

1 hermit = 1 bread
Bake: 10 minutes at 450°

	6	20	50	100
Crushed Whole Wheat Cereal	1/2 c	1 1/4 c	3 3/4 c	7 1/2 c
Grated Apples, unpeeled	1/4 c	2/3 c	1 2/3 c	3 1/3 c
Applesauce, unsweetened	1/4 c	2/3 c	1 2/3 c	3 1/3 c
Biscuit Mix, (p. 142)	1 c	2 1/8 c	5-1/3 c	10 2/3 c
Nutmeg	dash	1/8 t	1/2 t	1 t
Cinnamon	dash	1/8 t	1/2 t	1 t
Margarine				

1. Combine crushed cereal and apples in a bowl.
2. Pour applesauce over mixture.
3. Combine biscuit mix and spices. Add to apple mixture and mix well.
4. Drop by spoonfuls onto baking sheet greased with margarine.
5. Bake for 10-12 minutes at 450 degrees.

Note: Serve warm for best results. We do not recommend jam, jelly, or butter due to the sugar and fat content of these spreads. However, unsweetened apple butter complements these tasty rolls nicely.

PINEAPPLE AND BANANAS

$1/2$ cup = 1 fruit

	6	20	50	100
Pineapple Chunks, canned, undrained	$1^1/2$ c	3–1 lb cans	1–#10 can	2 #10 cans
Bananas, small	3	10	25	50

1. Slice bananas and combine with pineapple chunks and juice.

Note: This recipe can be made ahead of time. The acid in pineapple keeps the bananas from turning brown. Cover and refrigerate.

MACARONI BEEF AND CHEESE

1 serving = 1 meat; 1 bread
Bake: 20 minutes at 350°

	6	20	50	100
Ground Beef	8 oz	1 lb 8 oz	3 lb 12 oz	7 lb 8 oz
Spice Mix (p. 142)	1 t	1 T	2¹/₂ T	5 T
Dry Mustard	1 t	1 T	2¹/₂ T	5 T
Margarine	1¹/₂ T	5 T	³/₄ c	1¹/₂ c
Flour, enriched, or whole-grain	1¹/₂ T	5 T	³/₄ c	1¹/₂ c
Milk	³/₄ c	2¹/₄ c	6 c	12 c
Cheddar Cheese	4 oz	14 oz	2 lb 4 oz	4 lb 8 oz
Elbow Macaroni, dry	1¹/₈ c	3³/₄ c	7¹/₂ c	15 c
Bread Crumbs, whole-grain				

1. Brown ground beef in an iron skillet and drain fat.
2. Add spice mix and mustard and stir well.
3. Make thin white sauce by melting margarine and then gradually adding flour. Stir constantly. Slowly add milk, stirring until heated through.
4. Stir white sauce into meat.
5. Grate cheddar cheese and add to meat mixture, stirring thoroughly.
6. Cook macaroni according to directions on the box and drain.
7. Toss noodles with meat/cheese mixture until evenly mixed and then place in casserole or baking pan greased with cooking spray.
8. Sprinkle top with bread crumbs.
9. Cover and bake 15 minutes at 400 degrees. Remove cover and bake 5 minutes longer.
10. Divide into portions (approximately ³/₄ c per child) equal to number of children to be served.

Note: Use bread loaf ends to make bread crumbs by drying them in a warm oven. Let cool and chop in food processor.

STEAMED BROCCOLI

$^{1}/_{4}$ c = $^{1}/_{2}$ fruit/vegetable

See Quick Reference Chart, inside front cover, last page, and back cover, for amount needed.

1. Cut fresh broccoli into bite-size pieces. Include the stems and add a few broccoli leaves for extra iron.
2. Divide broccoli into 2 or 3 batches if cooking for a large group.
3. Steam broccoli until bright green and fork tender. If you plan to keep broccoli warm for later serving, slightly undercook.
4. Keep warm in 200 degree oven until ready to serve.

Note: If using frozen broccoli, prepare according to directions on package.

BREADSTICKS

1 breadstick = 1 bread
Bake: 15 minutes at 350°

	6	20	50	100
Yeast	½ t	2 t	1½ T	3 T
Flour, enriched or whole-grain	½ c	1½ c	3¾ c	7½ c
Milk	2 T	⅔ c	1⅔ c	3⅓ c
Water	2 t	¼ c	⅔ c	1⅓ c
Oil	1 T	3 T	⅓ c	¾ c + 1 T
Honey	2 t	2 T	¼ c	½ c
Cooking Spray				
Margarine				

1. Mix yeast with half the flour and set aside.
2. Heat milk, water, oil, and honey until warm, but not boiling.
3. Pour milk mixture into flour and yeast. Mix, then knead for three minutes.
4. Add remaining flour and mix with dough hook or by hand.
5. Allow dough to sit covered for 10 minutes.
6. Roll dough out on floured board to a thickness of ½".
7. Cut rolled dough into "sticks" six inches long.
8. Place on cookie sheet greased with cooking spray.
9. Cover with dry cloth and let rise 30 minutes.
10. Bake for 15 minutes at 350 degrees.
11. Brush tops with melted butter or margarine, if desired, to help keep breadsticks moist.

WEDNESDAY

MENU ITEM	SERVING SIZE=REQUIREMENT

BREAKFAST

Cereal, dry	$1/3$ c = 1 bread
Milk, fluid	$3/4$ c = 1 milk
Tomato Juice	$1/2$ c = 1 fruit

LUNCH/SUPPER

Ham and Cheese Sandwiches	$1/2$ sandwich = 1 meat; 1 bread
Raw Vegetables	$1/4$ c = $1/2$ fruit/vegetable
Ranch Dressing (optional)	
Finger Jello	1 serving = $1/2$ fruit/vegetable
Milk, fluid	$3/4$ c = 1 milk

SNACK

Pumpkin Cookies	1 cookie = 1 bread
Milk, fluid	$1/2$ c = 1 milk

Note: One Ham and Cheese Sandwich includes one meat requirement consisting of $2/3$ ham and $1/3$ cheese.

PLAN AHEAD TIP: Cook chicken for Thursday lunch/supper. See page 92.

HAM AND CHEESE SANDWICHES

$1/2$ sandwich = 1 meat; 1 bread

	6	20	50	100
Ham, 2 oz slices	6 oz (3 slices)	20 oz (10 slices)	3 lb 2 oz (25 slices)	6 lb 4 oz (50 slices)
American Cheese, 1 oz slices	3 oz (3 slices)	10 oz (10 slices)	1 lb 9 oz (25 slices)	3 lb 2 oz (50 slices)
Bread, whole-grain, thin-sliced	6	20	50	100

RAW VEGETABLES

$1/4$ c = $1/2$ fruit/vegetable

We suggest you use carrots, but any sliced vegetables will do as long as you have $1/4$ cup per child. See Quick Reference Chart, inside front cover, last page and inside back cover, for quantity information. Put a healthful dressing on the children's plates so they can "dip" their vegetables.

Note: Be sure to cut carrots into $1/4$" strips. Steam and chill the strips before serving. Slicing and steaming carrots reduces the chance that children will choke on them. See page 32 for more information on choking hazards.

FINGER GELATIN

1 serving = $1/2$ fruit/vegetable

	6	20	50	100
Grape Juice, 100% fruit	12 oz	5 c	3 qt + $1/2$ c	$1^1/2$ gal + 1 c
Gelatin	2 T	5 T	3/4 c + $1/2$ T	$1^1/2$ c + 1 T

1. Dissolve gelatin in juice and boil, stirring occasionally.
2. Pour gelatin into flat pan.
3. Refrigerate overnight.
4. Cut into equal portions and serve.

Note: This is the only way gelatin can be a reimbursable food on the CACFP. Jello brand gelatin is not reimbursable even when made with fruit juice.

PUMPKIN COOKIES

1 cookie = 1 bread
Bake: 15 minutes at 350°

	20	50	100
Sugar	1/3 c	1 c	2 c
Margarine, melted	1/3 c	1 1/4 c	3 c
Pumpkin	1/2 c	1 1/4 c	2 1/2 c
Egg, medium	1	2	4
Vanilla	1 t	3 t	6 t
Flour, enriched or whole-grain	1 1/4 c	3 c	6 c
Baking Soda	1/2 t	1 1/2 t	1 T
Baking Powder	1/2 t	1 1/2 t	1 T
Pumpkin Pie Spice	1/2 t	1 1/2 t	1 T
Cooking Spray			
Confectioners Sugar (optional)			

1. Mix sugar, margarine, pumpkin, egg, and vanilla.
2. Add dry ingredients.
3. Beat well. Dough should be stiff; add more flour if necessary.
4. Drop by spoonfuls onto a cookie sheet greased with cooking spray.
5. Bake at 350 degrees for 15 minutes.
6. Dust with confectioners sugar, if desired.

Note: If serving fewer than 20, refrigerate or freeze unused cookies to serve at a later date. See p. 44, for information about leftovers and frozen items.

WEDNESDAY WEDNESDAY WEDNESDAY WEDNESDAY WEDNESDAY WEDNESDAY

THURSDAY

MENU ITEM	SERVING SIZE=REQUIREMENT
	BREAKFAST
Cinnamon Toast	1 slice = 1 bread
Applesauce	½ c = 1 fruit
Milk, fluid	¾ c = 1 milk
	LUNCH
Chicken Spaghetti	1 serving = 1 meat; 1 bread
Peas and Carrots	¼ c = ½ fruit/vegetable
Fruit Cocktail	¼ c = ½ fruit/vegetable
Milk, fluid	¾ c = 1 milk
	SNACK
Bran Muffins	1 muffin = 1 bread
Apple Juice, with added vitamin C	½ c = 1 fruit

PLAN AHEAD TIP: Make Carrot and Raisin Salad and refrigerate for Friday. The salad tastes better when made a day ahead. See recipe on page 97.

CINNAMON TOAST

1 serving = 1 bread

	6	20	50	100
Margarine, softened	3 t	10 t	½ c	1 c
Bread, whole-grain, thin-sliced	6	20	50	100
Cinnamon	1½ t	5 t	¼ c	½ c
Sugar	1 T	3 T + 1 t	½ c + 1 t	1 c + 2 t

1. Spread ½ t margarine on one side of bread and place on pan, plain side down.
2. Combine cinnamon and sugar and stir until well blended.
3. Sprinkle cinnamon and sugar mixture onto bread with a shaker.
4. Place bread under broiler for 1 minute or until brown. Watch closely — cinnamon toast burns quickly.

CHICKEN SPAGHETTI

1 serving = 1 meat; 1 bread
BAKE: 20 MINUTES AT 375°

	6	20	50	100
Chicken, whole, uncooked	2 lb	5 lb 4 oz	13 lb	26 lb 2 oz
Thin Spaghetti Noodles, uncooked	6 oz	1 lb 8 oz	3 lb 2 oz	6 lb 2 oz
Chicken Bouillon, cubes or granules	1 cube (1 t)	3 cubes (3 t)	5/8 c	$1^{1}/4$ c
Hot Chicken Broth or Water	1 c	3 c	$7^{1}/2$ c	15 c
Cream of Chicken Soup, $10^{3}/4$ oz can	1 can	3 cans	7 cans	15 cans
Parmesan Cheese	2 T	6 T	1 c	2 c
Spice Mix (p. 142)	$^{1}/2$ T	2 T	$^{1}/3$ c	$^{2}/3$ c
Cooking Spray				

1. Place chicken in large soup pot and cover with water. Cover pan and bring to a boil. Lower heat and simmer chicken for 2 hours. Pour broth off chicken, reserving some for use in making bouillon.
2. Remove chicken from bones and dice. Be sure to discard the skin.
3. Cook spaghetti noodles as directed.
4. Dissolve bouillon in hot chicken broth or water.
5. Mix cream of chicken soup with broth.
6. Toss cooked chicken with Parmesan cheese and spice mix.
7. Add broth mixture to chicken and blend well.
8. Combine chicken and noodles and pour into casserole sprayed with cooking spray.
9. Bake at 375 degrees until bubbly, about 20 minutes.
10. Divide into portions (approximately $^{3}/4$ c per child) equal to number of children to be served.

Note: When you cook chicken, you can save the broth for later use in cooking vegetables, making soup base, or making bouillon. Cool broth in refrigerator and skim the fat. Then freeze the broth in handy amounts.

PEAS AND CARROTS

$1/4$ c = $1/2$ fruit/vegetable

	6	20	50	100
Green Peas, frozen	5 oz	1 lb	2 lb 8 oz	4 lb 12 oz
Carrots, fresh, without tops	5 oz	1 lb	2 lb 8 oz	4 lb 14 oz

1. Cook peas as directed.
2. Peel and thinly slice carrots.
3. Steam carrots for 8 minutes.
4. Toss cooked carrots and peas together.

BRAN MUFFINS

1 muffin = 1 bread
Bake: 15-20 minutes at 400°

Servings of regular-size muffins	36 ($^1/_2$ gal of batter)	72 (1 gal of batter)
Bran Flakes	2 c	4 c
Other Bran Cereal (100% bran)	1 c	2 c
Boiling Water	1 c	2 c
Buttermilk	1 pt	1 qt
Shortening	$^1/_2$ c	1 c
Sugar	1 c	2 c
Eggs, medium	3	6
Flour, enriched or whole-grain	$2^1/_2$ c	5 c
Baking soda	$2^1/_2$ t	5 t
Salt	$^1/_2$ t	1 t

1. Combine bran flakes, cereal, and boiling water in a bowl. Let stand for 20 minutes.
2. Stir in buttermilk.
3. In separate bowl, cream shortening and sugar together.
4. Add eggs to shortening mixture, one at a time, beating well after each addition. Add to bran mixture and mix well.
5. Sift flour, soda, and salt together. Stir into bran mixture until just mixed.
6. Cover and refrigerate until needed. Can be refrigerated for up to 30 days or frozen up to 2 months.
7. Coat muffin tin with cooking spray. Fill $^2/_3$ full with batter.
8. Bake muffins 15-20 minutes at 400 degrees.

Note: This is a great recipe that can be made ahead and used up to two months later. It actually improves with age. Large child care centers may want to make several gallons at a time. Family child care homes may want to make the amount for a half gallon of batter.

FRIDAY

MENU ITEM	SERVING SIZE=REQUIREMENT

BREAKFAST

Cereal, dry $\quad$ $\frac{1}{3}$ c = 1 bread

Grapes, quartered $\quad$ $\frac{3}{4}$ c = 1 fruit

Milk, fluid $\quad$ $\frac{3}{4}$ c = 1 milk

LUNCH/SUPPER

Hamburgers on a Roll $\quad$ 1 hamburger = 1 meat; 1 bread

Corn $\quad$ $\frac{1}{4}$ c = $\frac{1}{2}$ fruit/vegetable

Carrot and Raisin Salad $\quad$ $\frac{1}{4}$ c = $\frac{1}{2}$ fruit/vegetable (carrots = $\frac{1}{2}$)

Unsalted Potato Chips (optional)

Milk, fluid $\quad$ $\frac{3}{4}$ c = 1 milk

SNACK

Grape Juice $\quad$ $\frac{1}{2}$ c = 1 fruit

Vanilla Yogurt $\quad$ $\frac{1}{4}$ c = 1 meat

Animal Crackers $\quad$ 7 crackers= 1 bread (optional)

HAMBURGERS ON A ROLL

1 hamburger = 1 meat; 1 bread
Bake: 20-30 minutes at 400°

	6	20	50	100
Bread Crumbs	$^1/_3$ c	$^3/_4$ c	2 c	4 c
Water	$^1/_4$ c	1 c	2$^1/_2$ c	5 c
Eggs, medium	1	1	2	4
Spice Mix (p. 142)	1 t	1 T	3 T	6 T
Worcestershire Sauce	1 t	1 T	3 T	6 T
Ground Beef	12 oz	2 lb 10 oz	6 lb 9 oz	13 lb 7 oz
Hamburger Rolls, whole-grain	6	20	50	100

1. Combine first five ingredients and blend with mixer.
2. Add meat and stir. (Do not use hands.)
3. Scoop with #16 scoop (or $^1/_4$ cup measure) and shape into patties. Be sure to wear plastic gloves.
4. Place on flat pans. Bake 20-30 minutes at 400 degrees or until brown.
5. Put patties on buns. Stack in deep pan and cover with foil to keep warm until ready to serve.

CARROT AND RAISIN SALAD

$1/4$ c = $1/2$ fruit/vegetable

	6	20	50	100
Carrots, without tops, shredded	7 oz	1 lb 7 oz	3 lb 9 oz	7 lb 2 oz
Raisins	4 oz	11 oz	1 lb 10 oz	3 lb 4 oz
Crushed Pineapple, canned	$1^1/2$ T	$1/2$ c	$1^1/2$ c	3 c
Mayonnaise	$1/4$ c + 2 T	1 c	$2^1/2$ c	5 c

1. Soak raisins for 1 hour or more in pineapple juice drained from the crushed pineapple.
2. Drain raisins and combine all ingredients.
3. Chill (refrigerate overnight if possible) and serve.

CHAPTER SEVEN

MENUS AND RECIPES: WEEK THREE

WEEK THREE MENUS

Monday's Turkey Tetrazzini also tastes great made with tuna instead of turkey.

Tuesday's lunch includes mashed potatoes. Don't peel the potatoes, the potato skins contain Vitamin C.

Wednesday's lunch of Peanut Butter and Lettuce sandwiches is definitely different, but really tasty!

Thursday's afternoon snack of Whole Wheat Raisin Cookies can be made days earlier and frozen to save time.

Friday afternoon's snack includes Peanut Butter Pudding, which gives children some extra protein for the weekend.

WEEKLY MENU RECORD

Provider's Name _Alice_

	DAY/DATE	MON 10/15	TUE 10/16	WED 10/17	THUR 10/18	FRI 10/19
BREAKFAST	Fluid Milk	MILK	MILK		MILK	MILK
	Juice or Fruit or Vegetable	FRUIT-APPLES	ORANGE JUICE	PINEAPPLE CHUNKS	APPLES, SLICED	FR COCKTAIL
	Bread or Cereal or Alternate	RAISIN TOAST	OATMEAL/ RAISINS	WHOLE GRAIN BAGEL	CEREAL	TOAST
	Additional Foods (optional)	PEANUT BUTTER				
LUNCH/SUPPER	Fluid Milk	MILK	MILK	MILK	MILK	MILK
	Main Dish	TURKEY TETRAZINI		PB & LETTUCE SANDWICH	ITALIAN BAKE	SWEET & SOUR CHICKEN
	Meat or Alternate	TURKEY TETRAZINI	MEATLOAF	SANDWICH/ DEVILED EGG	ITALIAN BAKE	SWEET & SOUR CHICKEN
	Juice or Fruit or Vegetable	FR COCKTAIL	APPLE SAUCE MASHED POTATO	CARROTS/APPLES	ITALIAN BAKE/ PEARS	GR BEANS/ PEACHES
	Bread or Alternate	TURKEY TETRAZINI	BREAD	SANDWICH	ITALIAN BAKE/ BREAD	RICE
SNACK	Fluid Milk	BANANAS MILK	FISH CRACKERS	GRAHAM CRACKERS	WW RAISIN COOKIE	P.B. PUDDING APPLE JUICE
	Meat or Alternate				MILK	ANIMAL CRACKERS
	Juice or Fruit or Vegetable		APPLE JUICE	OJ		
	Bread or Cereal or Alternate					

MONDAY

MENU ITEM	SERVING SIZE=REQUIREMENT
	BREAKFAST
Raisin Toast, regular-slice	½ slice = 1 bread
Fruit, fresh, in season	½ c = 1 fruit
Milk, fluid	¾ c = 1 milk
Peanut Butter	1½ T = ½ meat (optional)
	LUNCH/SUPPER
Turkey Tetrazzini	1 serving = 1 bread; 1 meat
Steamed Broccoli and Cauliflower	¼ c = ½ fruit/vegetable
Fruit Cocktail	¼ c = ½ fruit/vegetable
Milk, Fluid	¾ c = 1 milk
	SNACK
Bananas, small	1 banana = 1 fruit
Milk, fluid	½ c = 1 milk

PLAN AHEAD TIP: Soak raisins overnight for Tuesday's breakfast oatmeal. See page 105.

TURKEY TETRAZZINI

1 serving = 1 bread; 1 meat
Bake: 20-25 minutes at 375°

	6	20	50	100
Noodles, flat vegetable	6 oz	1 lb 4 oz	3 lb 2 oz	6 lb 4 oz
Ground Turkey	1 lb	3 lb	7 lb	14 lb
Margarine	1 T	3 T	$1/4$ lb	$1/2$ lb
Onion, chopped	1 T	3 T	$1/2$ c	1 c
Cream of Mushroom Soup, $10\,3/4$ oz can	$1/2$ can	2 cans	5 cans	9 cans
Milk	$1/2$ c	2 c	$4^{1}/2$ c	9 c
Parmesan Cheese	3 T	$3/4$ c	$1^{1}/2$ c	3 c
Parsley, dried	1 T	3 T	$1/2$ c	1 c
Cooking Spray				

1. Cook noodles as directed and drain.
2. Brown ground turkey in iron skillet, chopping it into bite-size pieces as it cooks.
3. Remove turkey from pan and set aside. Melt margarine in pan and saute chopped onions until tender, but not brown.
4. Add soup, milk, and cheese to onion. Heat and stir.
5. Add parsley and turkey.
6. Toss noodles with turkey mixture.
7. Place into pans greased with cooking spray.
8. Cover with foil and bake at 375 degrees for 20-25 minutes or until heated through.
9. Divide into portions (approximately $3/4$ c per child) equal to number of children to be served.

STEAMED BROCCOLI AND CAULIFLOWER

$1/4$ c = $1/2$ fruit/vegetable

	6	20	50	100
Broccoli, fresh or frozen	6 oz	1 lb 1 oz	2 lb 10 oz	5 lb 3 oz
Cauliflower, fresh or frozen	6 oz	1 lb 3 oz	2 lb 14 oz	5 lb 11 oz

1. Cut vegetables into bite-size pieces. Include broccoli stems and add a few broccoli leaves, if desired. The leaves are rich in iron.
2. Divide broccoli and cauliflower pieces into 2 or 3 batches if cooking for a large group.
3. Steam broccoli until bright green and fork tender. Steam cauliflower until tender. Undercook if you are not serving within 10 minutes of cooking.
4. Keep warm in 200 degree oven until ready to serve.

Note: Prepare frozen broccoli and cauliflower according to directions on box.

TUESDAY

MENU ITEM	SERVING SIZE=REQUIREMENT
	BREAKFAST
Oatmeal with Raisins	$1/4$ c = 1 bread
Orange Juice	$1/2$ c = 1 fruit
Milk, fluid	$3/4$ c = 1 milk
	LUNCH/SUPPER
Meatloaf	1 serving = 1 meat
Mashed Potatoes	$1/4$ c = $1/2$ fruit/vegetable
Applesauce	$1/4$ c = $1/2$ fruit/vegetable
Bread, regular-slice	$1/2$ slice = 1 bread
Milk, fluid	$3/4$ c = 1 milk
	SNACK
Fish Crackers	32 crackers =1 bread
Juice, 100% fruit	$1/2$ c = 1 fruit

Note: One serving of meatloaf meets the requirement for one meat with $5/6$ beef and $1/6$ egg.

PLAN AHEAD TIP: Boil eggs for Deviled Eggs on Wednesday's lunch/supper. See page 109.

OATMEAL WITH RAISINS

$1/3$ c = 1 bread

	6	20	50	100
Raisins	$3/4$ c	$2^1/_2$ c	$6^1/_4$ c	$12^1/_2$ c
Water	$1^1/_3$ c	5 c	$12^1/_2$ c	25 c
Oats, quick or old fashioned	$2/3$ c	$2^3/_4$ c	$6^1/_2$ c	13 c
Margarine	1 T	3 T	$1/2$ c	1 c
Milk				

1. Soak raisins in water overnight.
2. Drain raisins, reserve water, and measure. Add tap water to equal recipe amount .
3. Put raisin water and oats in saucepan.
4. Cook over medium heat until boiling, stirring constantly.
5. Boil for 5 minutes, stirring occasionally. If using quick oats, cook 1 minute.
6. Remove from heat and add soaked raisins.
7. Add margarine and enough milk to thin oatmeal.

MEATLOAF

1 serving = 1 meat
Bake: 40 minutes at 350°

	6	20	50	100
Ground Beef	13 oz	3 lb	6 lb 12 oz	13 lb 8 oz
Tomato Sauce	$1/2$ c	$1^{1}/2$ c	$3^{3}/4$ c	$7^{1}/2$ c
Oats	$1/3$ c	1 c	$2^{1}/2$ c	5 c
Eggs, medium, beaten	1	3	6	12
Onion, chopped	1 T	$1/2$	1	2
Spice Mix (p. 142)	$1/2$ t	2 t	2 T	4 T
Salt	$1/2$ t	2 t	2 T	4 T

1. Mix all ingredients together.
2. Using wet hands, press meat mixture evenly into loaf pan(s).
3. Bake at 350 degrees for 40 minutes.
4. Cut into portions equal to number of children to be served.

Note: To give the meatloaf color, spread ketchup over the top immediately after cooking. This also helps to keep the meatloaf moist while waiting to be served.

MASHED POTATOES

$^1/_4$ c = $^1/_2$ fruit/vegetable

	6	20	50	100
White Potatoes, fresh, unpeeled	15 oz	3 lb	7 lb 6 oz	14 lb 12 oz
Water	1$^1/_4$ c	1 qt	2$^1/_2$ qt	1 gal + 1 qt
Milk, heated	3 oz	$^3/_4$ c	1$^3/_4$ c	3$^1/_2$ c
Margarine, softened	1 T	$^1/_4$ c	$^1/_2$ c	1 c

1. Scrub potatoes well and cut into quarters.
2. Boil potatoes about 25 minutes until tender. Drain.
3. Mash potatoes in mixer on low speed until smooth.
4. Gradually, add just enough milk to moisten.
5. Add margarine while beating on low speed.
6. Mix on high speed until blended and potatoes are light and fluffy.
7. Serve with a #16 scoop ($^1/_4$ c).

WEDNESDAY

MENU ITEM	SERVING SIZE=REQUIREMENT

BREAKFAST

Bagels, enriched or whole-grain	½ bagel = 1 bread
Pineapple Chunks	½ c = 1 fruit
Milk, fluid	¾ c = 1 milk

LUNCH/SUPPER

Peanut Butter & Lettuce Sandwiches	1 sandwich = ½ meat; 1 bread
Deviled Eggs	½ egg = ½ meat
Apples or Bananas	¼ c = ½ fruit/vegetable
Carrot Sticks	¼ c = ½ fruit/vegetable
Milk, fluid	¾ c = 1 milk

SNACK

Graham Crackers	3 crackers = 1 bread
Orange Juice, 100 % fruit	½ c = 1 fruit

PLAN AHEAD TIP: Cook tomato sauce for Italian Bake to be served at Thursday lunch/supper. See page 111.

PEANUT BUTTER & LETTUCE SANDWICHES

1 sandwich = 1/2 meat; 1 bread

	6	20	50	100
Peanut Butter	9 T	1 lb + 1^{1}/$_{2}$ T	2^{1}/$_{2}$ lb + 1^{1}/$_{2}$ T	5 lb + 3 T
Lettuce Leaves				
Bread, thin-sliced	12	40	100	200

DEVILED EGGS

1/4 egg = 1/2 meat

	6	20	50	100
Eggs, medium	3	10	25	50
Mayonnaise	1/4 c	3/4 c + 1 T	2 c	4 c
Relish	1/4 c	3/4 c + 1 T	2 c	4 c

1. Boil eggs and refrigerate until cool throughout.
2. Peel eggs, slice lengthwise, and remove yolks.
3. Mix yolks with mayonnaise and relish.
4. Fill egg halves with yolk mixture.

CARROTS

1/4 c = 1/2 fruit/vegetable

See Quick Reference Chart, inside front cover, last page, and inside back cover, for amount needed.

Note: Be sure to cut carrots into 1/4" strips. Steam and chill the strips before serving. Slicing and steaming carrots reduces the chance that children will choke on them. See page 32 for more information about choking hazards.

THURSDAY

MENU ITEM	SERVING SIZE=REQUIREMENT
	BREAKFAST
Cereal, dry	$^1/_2$ c = 1 bread
Apples, sliced	$^1/_2$ c = 1 fruit
Milk, fluid	$^3/_4$ c = 1 milk
	LUNCH/SUPPER
Italian Bake	1 serving = 1 meat; $^1/_2$ bread; $^1/_2$ fruit/vegetable
Pears, canned	$^1/_4$ c = $^1/_2$ fruit/vegetable
Bread, thin-sliced	$^1/_2$ slice = $^1/_2$ bread
Milk, fluid	$^3/_4$ c = 1 milk
	SNACK
Whole Wheat Raisin Cookies	1 cookie = 1 bread
Juice, 100% fruit	$^1/_2$ c = 1 fruit

PLAN AHEAD TIP: Cook chicken for Sweet and Sour Chicken to be served Friday. See page 115.

ITALIAN BAKE

1 serving = 1 meat; 1/2 bread
Bake: 20 minutes at 350°

	6	20	50	100
Garlic Powder	1 T	1/4 c	2/3 c	1 1/3 c
Tomatoes, canned	16 oz can	2–28 oz cans	1–#10 + 1–16 oz cans	2 #10 + 2 16-oz cans
Tomato Paste	6-oz can	4–6 oz cans	2–#2 1/2 cans	1–#10 can
Water	6 oz	2 1/2 c	1 1/2 qt + 1/4 c	3 qt + 1/2 c
Ketchup	1/3 c	1 c	2 3/4 c	5 1/2 c
Worcestershire Sauce	1 T	1/4 c	2/3 c	1 1/3 c
Macaroni	5 oz	1 lb	2 lb 8 oz	5 lb
Onions, chopped	2 T	1 whole	3 whole	6 whole
Ground Beef	1 lb	3 lb	7 lb	14 lb
Parmesan Cheese	1/4 c	1 c	2 1/2 c	5 c

1. To make tomato sauce, combine first six ingredients in a sauce pan. Simmer for 4-6 hours, stirring occasionally to prevent sticking.
2. Cook macaroni as directed and drain.
3. Chop onions and put in cast iron skillet.
4. Add ground beef, mixing well with onions. Saute until browned, breaking meat into small bite-size pieces. Drain off fat.
5. Place meat and macaroni in baking pan, combine well.
6. Add tomato sauce and stir well.
7. Sprinkle top with Parmesan Cheese.
8. Bake at 350 degrees for 20 minutes or until bubbly.
9. Divide into portions (approximately 3/4 cup per child) equal to number of children to be served.

(continued on next page)

Note: You can be creative when selecting pasta for this recipe. Children like spirals, bows, rigatoni, etc. The amounts indicated are given by weight so it will not vary from one kind of pasta to another.

To save time, buy prepared spaghetti sauce. You will need the following amount of sauce to meet ½ fruit/vegetable requirement:

	6	20	50	100
Spaghetti Sauce	1–16 oz can	3½–16 oz cans	1–#10 can	2–#10 cans

RAISIN COOKIES

1 cookie = 1 bread
Bake: 9 minutes at 350°

	50	100
Flour, enriched or whole-grain	2 c	4 c
Baking Powder	1½ t	1 T
Cinnamon	½ t	1 t
Brown Sugar, packed	⅓ c	⅔ c
Vegetable Shortening	⅔ c	1⅓ c
Eggs, medium	1	2
Milk	¼ c	½ c
Vanilla	1 t	2 t
Applesauce	½ c	1 c
Raisins	1 c	2 c
Cooking Spray		

1. Mix flour, baking powder, and cinnamon. Set aside.
2. Cream sugar and shortening.
3. Add egg, milk, vanilla, and applesauce to creamed mixture. Mix well.
4. Stir in dry ingredients. Add raisins and mix well.
5. Drop by teaspoonful one inch apart onto baking sheet greased with cooking spray.
6. Bake 9 minutes at 350 degrees.

Note: We recommend that you make at least 50 cookies and freeze unused portions to serve at a later date. See p. 44 for information about leftovers and frozen items.

FRIDAY

MENU ITEM   **SERVING SIZE=REQUIREMENT**

BREAKFAST

Toast, thin-sliced   1 slice = 1 bread
Fruit Cocktail $\frac{1}{2}$ c = 1 fruit/vegetable
Milk, fluid $\frac{3}{4}$ c = 1 milk

LUNCH/SUPPER

Sweet & Sour Chicken   1 serving = 1 meat
Rice $\frac{1}{4}$ c = 1 bread
French Green Beans $\frac{1}{4}$ c = $\frac{1}{2}$ fruit/vegetable
Peaches, canned $\frac{1}{4}$ c = $\frac{1}{2}$ fruit/vegetable
Milk, fluid $\frac{3}{4}$ c = 1 milk

SNACK

Peanut Butter Pudding $\frac{1}{4}$ c = 1 meat
Apple Juice, with added Vitamin C, 100% fruit $\frac{1}{4}$ c = $\frac{1}{2}$ fruit/vegetable
Animal Crackers   7 crackers= 1 bread (optional)

SWEET & SOUR CHICKEN

1 serving = 1 meat
Bake: 20 minutes at 375°

	6	20	50	100
Chicken, whole, uncooked	2 lb	5 lb 4 oz	13 lb 1 oz	26 lb 2 oz
Ketchup	¼ c	1¼ c	3 c	1½ qt
Water	¼ c + 1 T	1 c	2½ c	5 c
Honey	2 T	½ c	1¼ c	2½ c
Tomato Sauce	¼ c	¾ c	2 c	4 c
Worcestershire Sauce	½ t	1¼ t	1 T	2 T
Vinegar	½ t	1¼ t	1 T	2 T
Cornstarch	1½ t	5 t	¼ c	½ c
Water	1 T	2 T + 2 t	¼ c	¾ c
Cooking Spray				

1. Place chicken in large soup pot and cover with water. Cover pan and bring to a boil. Lower heat and simmer chicken for 2 hours. Pour broth off chicken, reserving some for cooking the rice. Be sure to cool broth and skim off fat before using.
2. Remove chicken from bones and discard skin. Shred meat and set aside. (See p. 32 about choking hazards.)
3. Mix ketchup, first water amount, honey, tomato sauce, Worcestershire sauce, and vinegar in a sauce pan.
4. Heat until boiling.
5. Mix cornstarch with second water amount. Add to tomato sauce mixture.
6. Boil until thickened and add cooked chicken. Stir well.
7. Pour all into casserole greased with cooking spray.
8. Bake at 350 degrees for 45 minutes.
9. Divide into portions (approximately ¼ c per child) equal to the number of children to be served.

RICE

$1/4$ c = 1 bread

See Quick Reference Chart, inside front cover, last page, and inside back cover, for amount of rice to purchase and prepare.

1. Cook rice as directed, using chicken broth in place of water. Do not add salt or margarine.

FRENCH GREEN BEANS

$1/4$ c = $1/2$ fruit/vegetable

	6	20	50	100
Frozen Green Beans, French Style	8 oz	1 lb 12 oz	4 lb 4 oz	8 lb 8 oz
Minced Dry Onion	2 t	1½ T	¼ c	½ c
Spice Mix (p. 142)	1 t	1 T	¼ c	½ c
Chicken Bouillon Cubes	1	2	4	8
Hot Water	1 c	2 c	4 c	8 c

1. Dissolve bouillon cubes in hot water.
2. Add spices, onion, and frozen green beans.
3. Cook until tender, using package directions.
4. Drain and serve.

Note: Below is a recipe for canned, regular-cut beans in case you have them in your pantry.

GREEN BEANS, REGULAR-CUT

$1/4$ c = $1/2$ fruit/vegetable

See Quick Reference Chart for amount of regular-cut green beans to purchase and prepare.

1. Drain liquid from canned beans and rinse.
2. Put beans in pot and add water just to cover.
3. Add chicken bouillon cube(s).
4. Bring beans to a boil and let simmer until time to serve.

PEANUT BUTTER PUDDING

¹/₄ c = 1 meat

	20	50	100
Peanut Butter, natural	²/₃ c	1¹/₂ c	3 c
Sugar	²/₃ c	1¹/₂ c	3 c
Salt	dash	¹/₂ t	1 t
Hot Milk	1 qt	2¹/₂ qt	1 gal + 1 qt
Eggs	1	4	8
Water	¹/₈ c	¹/₂ c	1 c
Cornstarch	¹/₃ c	³/₄ c	1¹/₂ c
Vanilla	2 t	2 T	¹/₄ c

1   Add sugar and salt to milk and peanut butter; heat to simmering point.
2   Beat eggs; combine with water. Beat in cornstarch.
3   Add egg mixture slowly to milk mixture, stirring constantly with a whip. Cook about 6 minutes, continuing to stir, until mixture has returned to simmering point.
4   Remove pudding from heat and stir in vanilla.
5   Cool quickly in the refrigerator, stirring often.

Note: If serving fewer than 20, save leftovers for a snack later next week.

CHAPTER EIGHT

MENUS AND RECIPES: WEEK FOUR

WEEK FOUR MENUS

Monday's Lasagna recipe shows you a preparation short cut. This recipe uses uncooked lasagna noodles!

Tuesday's simple afternoon snack will allow you extra time to cook chicken for Wednesday's lunch.

Wednesday's Bueno Bean Soup is simple and quick. Adults like it when served cold with a spoonful of sour cream on top!

Thursday's breakfast includes pancakes, which are a favorite with children. Lunch is a vegetarian meal.

Friday afternoon's menu includes Rice Cakes. There are many varieties of rice cakes available; some with popcorn added, some with sesame seeds. Try them all!

WEEKLY MENU RECORD

Provider's Name _Alice_

	DAY/DATE	MON 10/22	TUE 10/23	WED 10/24	THURS 10/25	FRI 10/26
BREAKFAST	Fluid Milk	MILK	MILK	MILK	MILK	MILK
	Juice or Fruit or Vegetable	APPLE JUICE	ORANGES	ORANGE JUICE	PINEAPPLE	
	Bread or Cereal or Alternate	TOAST	CEREAL	BRAN MUFFIN	PANCAKES	TOAST
	Additional Foods (optional)	SCRAMBLED EGG				
LUNCH/SUPPER	Fluid Milk	MILK	MILK	MILK	MILK	MILK
	Main Dish	LASAGNA		CHICKEN SALAD SANDWICH	MAC & CHEESE	TACO BAKE
	Meat or Alternate	LASAGNA	HAM & CHEESE PIE	CHICKEN SALAD SANDWICH BEAN SOUP	MAC & CHEESE BAKED BEANS	TACO BAKE
	Juice or Fruit or Vegetable	APPLE SAUCE/ PEAS	LIMA BEANS/ PINEAPPLE	BEAN SOUP/ APPLE SLICES	FR COCKTAIL	APPLESAUCE/ TACO BAKE
	Bread or Alternate	LASAGNA/ GARLIC/ TOAST	BREAD		MAC & CHEESE	TACO BAKE
SNACK	Fluid Milk	LEMON COOKIES	BUTTER CRACKERS PEANUT BUTTER	GRAHAM CRACKERS	CREAM CHEESE/ PINEAPPLE SANDWICH	APPLE JUICE/ RICE CAKES/ AMERICAN CHEESE
	Meat or Alternate	MILK	APPLE JUICE	FRUIT FLIP	OJ	
	Juice or Fruit or Vegetable					
	Bread or Cereal or Alternate					

120 CHILD CARE COOKBOOK

MONDAY

MENU ITEM	SERVING SIZE=REQUIREMENT
	BREAKFAST
Toast, regular-sliced	$^1/_2$ slice = 1 bread
Juice, 100% fruit	$^1/_2$ c = 1 fruit
Milk, fluid	$^3/_4$ c = 1 milk
Scrambled Eggs	2 T = $^1/_2$ meat(optional)
	LUNCH/SUPPER
Lasagna	1 serving = 1 meat ; $^1/_2$ bread
Applesauce	$^1/_4$ c = $^1/_2$ fruit/vegetable
Peas	$^1/_4$ c = $^1/_2$ fruit/vegetable
Garlic Toast, thin-sliced	$^1/_2$ slice = $^1/_2$ bread
Milk, fluid	$^3/_4$ c = 1 milk
	SNACK
Lemon Cookies	1 cookie = 1 bread
Milk, fluid	$^1/_2$ c = 1 milk

Note: One serving of Lasagna meets CACFP requirements for 1 meat ($^1/_2$ beef and $^1/_2$ cheese and egg) and $^1/_2$ bread (noodles).

SCRAMBLED EGGS

2 T = $^1/_2$ meat (optional)

	6	20	50	100
Whole Eggs, medium	3	10	25	50
Milk	$^1/_4$ c	$^3/_4$ c	2 c	4 c
Onion Powder	pinch	$^1/_2$ t	$1^1/_2$ t	3 t

1. Beat eggs, milk, and onion powder together in large bowl.
2. Preheat non-stick griddle.
3. Pour egg mixture onto griddle.
4. Stir and mix when egg begins to cook.

Note: Remember to undercook eggs slightly if it is not time to serve them yet. This way they will not be overcooked if you keep them warm in the oven.

LASAGNA

1 serving = 1 meat; ½ bread
Bake: 1½ hours at 350°

	6	20	50	100
Ground Beef	4 oz	13 oz	2 lb	4 lb
Onions, chopped	2 t	2 T	½ c	1 c
Garlic Powder	¾ t	2½ t	2 T	3 T
Spice Mix (p. 142)	pinch	1 t	1 T	2 T
Cottage Cheese, low-fat	4 oz	13 oz	2 lb	4 lb
Eggs, medium	1	2	4	7
Parmesan Cheese	2 T	⅓ c	1 c	2 c
Parsley	2 t	2 T	¼ c	½ c
Tomato Sauce	1–8 oz can	2–15 oz cans	2–#2½ cans	1–#10 can
Water	½ c	1½ c	1 qt	2 qt
Mozzarella Cheese, shredded	4 oz	13 oz	2 lb	4 lb
Lasagna Noodles	7 noodles	11 noodles	1 lb 8 oz	3 lb

1. Brown ground beef in iron skillet; drain fat.
2. Add chopped onions, garlic powder, and spice mix to beef.
3. In separate bowl combine cottage cheese, eggs, Parmesan cheese, and parsley.
4. Combine tomato sauce and water, and add to ground beef mixture.
5. Put enough meat sauce in pan to cover the bottom.
6. Repeat the following layers three times: uncooked noodles, cheese mixture, mozzarella cheese, meat sauce.
7. Cover entire pan tight with foil so no steam escapes.
8. Bake at 350 degrees for 1 hour 15 minutes. Remove foil and cook 10-15 minutes more.

GARLIC TOAST

$^1/_2$ slice = $^1/_2$ bread

	6	20	50	100
Garlic Powder	1 t	1 T + 1 t	3 T	$^1/_4$ c + 2 T
Margarine	2 T	$^1/_3$ c	1 c	2 c
Parmesan Cheese	1 T	3 T	$^1/_2$ c	1 c

1. Remove bread from package, keeping loaf together. Slice bread lengthwise through the middle.
2. Melt margarine over low heat.
3. Add garlic powder and Parmesan cheese to melted margarine.
4. Drip margarine mixture over cut edges of each half.
5. Wrap in foil and heat in oven with lasagna during last 10 minutes.

Note: See Quick Reference Chart, inside front cover, last page, and inside back cover, for bread quantities.

LEMON COOKIES

1 cookie = 1 bread
Bake: 7 MINUTES at 400°

	20	50	100
Margarine	6 T	8 oz	1 lb
Sugar	$^1/_3$ c	1 c	2 c
Eggs	1	2	4
Lemon Extract	1 t	1 T	2 T
Lemon Rind, grated	$^1/_2$ t	2 t	4 t
Flour	$1^1/_4$ c	3 c	6 c
Salt	2 dash	1 t	2 t
Baking Powder	$^3/_4$ t	$1^1/_2$ t	1 T
Cooking Spray			

1. Cream together margarine and sugar.
2. Add eggs, lemon extract, and lemon rind. Mix well.
3. Gradually add flour, salt, and baking powder, mixing well after each addition.
4. Roll dough about $^1/_4$ inch thick on lightly floured board.
5. Cut with two-inch cookie cutter and place on cookie sheet greased with cooking spray.
6. Bake 7 minutes at 400 degrees.

Note: These cookies freeze well. Make at least 20 and freeze the extras for another day's snack.

PLAN AHEAD TIP: You can make this recipe ahead of time up to step 4. Just roll dough into log, wrap in wax paper and freeze. When you are ready to bake just remove from freezer, take off wax paper and slice off cookies, about $^1/_4$" thick.

TUESDAY

MENU ITEM	SERVING SIZE=REQUIREMENT
	BREAKFAST
Cereal	$^1/_3$ c = 1 bread
Fruit	$^1/_2$ c = 1 fruit
Milk, fluid	$^3/_4$ c = 1 milk
	LUNCH/SUPPER
Ham & Cheese Pie	1 serving = 1 meat
Lima Beans	$^1/_4$ c = $^1/_2$ vegetable
Pineapple	$^1/_4$ c = $^1/_2$ fruit/vegetable
Bread, thin-sliced	1 slice = 1 bread
Milk, fluid	$^3/_4$ c = 1 milk
	SNACK
Butter Crackers and Peanut Butter	8 crackers= 1 bread
Juice, 100% fruit	$^1/_2$ c = 1 fruit

Note: Ham and Cheese Pie meets CACFP requirements for 1 meat serving with $^1/_2$ ham and $^1/_2$ cheese and eggs.

PLAN AHEAD TIP: If you have bran muffin batter (recipe on p. 94) stored in the freezer, thaw muffin batter overnight for Wednesday's breakfast. Cook chicken for Wednesday's lunch and refrigerate.

HAM AND CHEESE PIE

1 serving = 1 meat
Bake: 40 minutes at 400°

	6	20	50	100
Cooking Spray				
Eggs, medium	2	6	15	30
Milk	1 c	3 c	7½ c	15 c
Biscuit Mix (p. 142)	½ c	1½ c	3¾ c	7½ c
Spice Mix (p. 142)	1 t	1 T	¼ c	½ c
Ham, boneless, canned	12 oz	2 lb	5 lb	10 lb
Monterey Jack Cheese, grated	½ c	2 c	5 c	10 c

1. Lightly coat pan with cooking spray.
2. Mix eggs, milk, biscuit mix, and spice mix together. Mix with beater or blender in smaller portions.
3. Shred ham in food processor and put in bottom of pan.
4. Grate cheese and sprinkle over ham.
5. Pour egg mixture over ham and cheese.
6. Bake for 40 minutes at 400 degrees.
7. Let sit for 15 minutes before cutting into serving sizes.

Note: Just about any cheese will taste fine in this casserole. Mixing some shredded cheddar with the Monterey Jack gives a different flavor.

TUESDAY TUESDAY TUESDAY TUESDAY TUESDAY TUESDAY TUESDAY TUESDAY

PEANUT BUTTER AND CRACKERS

8 crackers = 1 bread

See amounts in Quick Reference Chart, inside fron cover, last page, and inside back cover.

We have proposed providing enough crackers to meet one full bread requirement, so peanut butter is optional. You can let the children spread their own peanut butter since it does not matter how much they eat.

If you cut back on the number of crackers and use peanut butter to meet half the snack requirement, you must measure it and put the correct amount on each cracker. Therefore an adult, not the children, must spread the peanut butter.

WEDNESDAY

MENU ITEM

SERVING SIZE=REQUIREMENT

BREAKFAST

Bran Muffins with Fruit
Juice, 100% fruit
Milk, fluid

1 muffin = 1 bread
$\frac{1}{2}$ c = 1 fruit
$\frac{3}{4}$ c = 1 milk

LUNCH/SUPPER

Chicken Salad Sandwiches
Bueno Bean Soup
Fruit Slices
Milk, fluid

1 sandwich = 1 bread; $\frac{1}{2}$ meat
$\frac{3}{4}$ c = $\frac{1}{2}$ meat; $\frac{1}{2}$ fruit/vegetable
$\frac{1}{4}$ c = $\frac{1}{2}$ fruit/vegetable
$\frac{3}{4}$ c = 1 milk

SNACK

Jo's Fruit Flip
Graham Crackers

$\frac{3}{4}$ c = $\frac{1}{2}$ milk; $\frac{1}{2}$ fruit
3 crackers= 1 bread

BRAN MUFFINS WITH FRUIT

1 muffin = 1 bread
Bake: 20 minutes at 400°

	6	20	50	100
Fruit	$^1/_3$ c	1 c	$2^1/_2$ c	5 c

1. Make bran muffin batter (p. 94) or thaw stored batter.
2. Chop dried fruit of choice (apricots, dates, etc.) or wash fresh blueberries. Mix with batter.
3. Spray muffin tins with non-stick vegetable oil spray.
4. Fill muffin tins $^2/_3$ full with batter.
5. Bake for 20 minutes at 400 degrees.

CHICKEN SALAD SANDWICHES

1 sandwich = 1 bread; $^1/_2$ meat

	6	20	50	100
Chicken, whole	1 lb	3 lb	6 lb 8 oz	13 lb
Mayonnaise, reduced-fat	2 T	$^2/_3$ c	$1^1/_3$ c	$2^2/_3$ c
Sweet Relish	2 T	$^2/_3$ c	$1^1/_3$ c	$2^2/_3$ c
Bread, thin-sliced	12	40	100	200

1. Place chicken in large soup pot and cover with water. Cover pan and bring to a boil. Lower heat and simmer chicken for 2 hours. Pour broth off chicken, reserving it for use in making Bueno Bean Soup. Be sure to skim fat before using broth.
2. Pull chicken from bones, discarding the skin. Chop meat into small pieces; a food processor works well for this task.
3. Put cooled chicken meat, mayonnaise, and relish in large bowl. Mix well.
4. Spread on bread, using $^1/_4$ cup or #16 scoop to measure each serving.

Note: This makes an excellent pasta salad when you add spiral noodles. See Quick Reference Chart on inside front cover, last page, and inside back cover for pasta quantities.

BUENO BEAN SOUP

$3/4$ c = $1/2$ meat; $1/2$ fruit/vegetable

	6	20	50	100
Stewed Tomatoes	1–14$1/2$ oz can	3$1/2$-14$1/2$ oz cans	1–#10 can	2–#10 cans
Water or Chicken Broth	1$1/2$ c	5 c	12$1/2$ c	6 qt + 1 c
Chicken Bouillon, cube or granules	1 cube	3 cubes	$5/8$ c or 10 cubes	1$1/4$ c or 20 cubes
Refried Beans	16 oz can	3$1/2$-16 oz cans	1–#10 can	2–#10 cans

1. Puree stewed tomatoes in blender or food processor.
2. Combine tomatoes, water or broth, and chicken bouillon in pan.
3. Simmer until bouillon is dissolved.
4. Add refried beans.
5. Stir well and heat through.

JO'S FRUIT FLIP

$^3/_4$ c = $^1/_2$ milk; $^1/_2$ fuit

	6	20	50	100
Bananas	1	3$^1/_3$	8$^2/_3$	16$^1/_3$
Milk	1$^1/_2$ c	5 c	12$^1/_2$ c	50 c
Pineapple Juice	$^3/_4$ c	2$^1/_2$ c	6$^1/_4$ c	12$^1/_2$ c

1. Put all ingredients into a blender. (Make in small batches.)
2. Blend on high for 1 minute.
3. Divide into $^3/_4$ cup servings and serve immediately, or stir well before serving later.

THURSDAY

MENU ITEM	SERVING SIZE=REQUIREMENT
	BREAKFAST
Pancakes	2 pancakes= 1 bread
Fruit	½ c = 1 fruit
Milk, fluid	¾ c = 1 milk
	LUNCH/SUPPER
Macaroni and Cheese	½ c = 1 bread; ½ meat
Baked Beans	¼ c = ½ meat
Broccoli	¼ c = ½ fruit/vegetable
Fruit Cocktail	¼ c = ½ fruit/vegetable
Milk, fluid	¾ c = 1 milk
	SNACK
Cream Cheese with Pineapple Sandwiches	½ sandwich = 1 bread
Juice, 100% fruit	½ c = 1 fruit

PANCAKES

2 pancakes = 1 bread

	6	20	50	100
Biscuit Mix (p. 142)	2 c	6$\frac{1}{4}$ c	15$\frac{1}{2}$ c	31 c
Milk	1 c	3$\frac{1}{8}$ c	2 qt	1 gal
Eggs, medium	1	3	6	12

1. Combine biscuit mix, milk, and eggs in large bowl.
2. Mix thoroughly until smooth, using wire whip.
3. Lightly grease griddle with oil or use non-stick griddle.
4. Use $\frac{1}{4}$ cup measure to pour batter onto hot griddle.
5. Turn pancakes when sides appear dry and bubbles break on top.
6. Keep warm in 200 degree oven until ready to serve.

MACARONI AND CHEESE

$1/2$ c = 1 bread; $1/2$ meat
Bake: 15 minutes at 375°

	6	20	50	100
Elbow Macaroni, dry, enriched	6 oz	1 lb + 2 T	2 lb 10 oz	5 lb 4 oz
Cooking Spray				
Margarine	$1^1/_2$ T	5 T	$^3/_4$ c	$1^1/_2$ c
Flour, enriched or whole-grain	2 T	$^1/_3$ c	$^3/_4$ c	$1^1/_2$ c
Milk	$^2/_3$ c	$2^1/_3$ c	6 c	12 c
Dry Mustard	$^1/_4$ t	$^1/_2$ t	$1^1/_2$ t	1 T
Worcestershire Sauce	$^1/_4$ t	$^1/_2$ t	$1^1/_2$ t	1 T
Spice Mix (p. 142)	$^1/_4$ t	$^1/_2$ t	$1^1/_2$ t	1 T
Cheddar Cheese	4 oz	11 oz	1 lb 11 oz	3 lb 6 oz

1. Cook macaroni as directed. Drain. Put in pan sprayed with cooking spray.
2. Melt margarine over low heat. Add flour and milk, stirring constantly to avoid lumps.
3. Stir in dry mustard, Worcestershire, and spice mix.
4. Grate cheddar cheese.
5. Add half the grated cheese to the sauce and stir until melted.
6. Add sauce to macaroni and mix well.
7. Fold in the rest of the cheese.
8. Cook at 375 degrees for 15 minutes.

CREAM CHEESE WITH PINEAPPLE SANDWICHES

1/2 sandwich = 1 bread

	6	*20*	*50*	*100*
Cream Cheese	1 1/2 T	1/2 c	1 1/2 c	3 c
Crushed Pineapple, canned	1 1/2 T	1/2 c	1 1/2 c	3 c
Bread, regular slice	6	20	50	100

1. Drain pineapple, reserving juice.
2. Mix cream cheese and pineapple together with a hand mixer. Use reserved juice to thin cream cheese, if necessary. Cream cheese should be thin enough to spread easily on bread.
3. Spread on bread, top with another slice of bread and cut into fourths. To make sandwiches look festive, remove crust and cut each sandwich into four triangles.

FRIDAY

MENU ITEM	SERVING SIZE=REQUIREMENT

BREAKFAST

Toast, regular-slice 🥕	½ slice = 1 bread
Applesauce 🥕	½ c = 1 fruit
Milk, fluid 🥕	¾ c = 1 milk

LUNCH/SUPPER

Taco Bake	1 serving = 1 bread; 1 meat
Tossed Salad	¼ c = ½ fruit/vegetable
Applesauce	¼ c = ½ fruit/vegetable
Milk, fluid 🥕	¾ c = 1 milk

SNACK

American Cheese	½ oz = 1 meat
Apple Juice with Vitamin C added, 100% fruit juice 🥕	½ c = 1 fruit
Rice Cakes, whole-grain	1 = ½ bread (optional)

TACO BAKE

1 serving = 1 bread; 1 meat
Bake: 45 minutes at 350°

	6	20	50	100
Onion, whole	¼	1	2	4
Taco Seasoning	¾ t	1½ T	3 T	6 T
Tomato Sauce	½ c	1¼ c	2–#303 cans	4–#303 cans
Refried Beans	16 oz can	3–16 oz cans	1–#10 can	2–#10 cans
Biscuit Mix, (p. 142)	⅓ c	2 c	4½ c	9 c
Yellow Cornmeal	¼ c	⅔ c	1½ c	3 c
Milk	3 T	½ c	1 c	2 c
Eggs, medium, beaten	1	2	5	9
Oil	2 T	6 T	½ c	1 c
Cooking Spray				
Cheddar Cheese, shredded	4 oz	12 oz	2 lb 4 oz	4 lb 8 oz
Sour Cream, reduced-fat	⅔ c	1¾ c	4½ c	9 c
Eggs	1	2	5	9

1. Chop onions in food processor.
2. Combine and heat onions, seasoning mix, tomato sauce, and refried beans in cast iron skillet.
3. In separate bowl, combine biscuit mix, cornmeal, milk, first eggs (beaten), and oil until moistened. Beat vigorously for 30 seconds.
4. Spray pan with cooking spray and spread cornmeal mixture to cover the bottom.
5. Spoon bean mixture over dough and spread evenly.
6 Shred cheddar cheese and mix with sour cream and second eggs.
7. Spread sour cream mixture on top of bean mixture.
8. Bake 45 minutes at 350 degrees. Let stand 15 minutes before cutting.
9. Cut into portions equal to number of children to be served.

TOSSED SALAD

½ c = ½ fruit/vegetable

	6	20	50	100
Lettuce, shredded	1½ c	5 c	2 lb	4 lb
Tomatoes, whole	¼	1	2	4
Cucumbers, whole	¼	½	1½	3
Salad Dressing, low-fat				

1. Rinse vegetables.
2. Chop in small pieces.
3. Toss together.
4. Serve with low-fat salad dressing.

RICE CAKES WITH CHEESE

1 = ½ bread

	6	20	50	100
Rice Cakes, whole-grain	6	20	50	100
American Cheese, 1 oz slices	3	10	25	50

1. Cut slices of cheese in half. Cutting a whole stack of cheese at once will speed this process.
2. Place one-half slice of cheese on each rice cake.
3. Place under broiler until cheese is melted, 1 minute or less.
4. Serve one rice cake per child.

Note: Rice cakes are optional in this menu, but if you decide to serve them, combine with cheese to make a tasty snack.

CHAPTER NINE

CHOICES AND SUBSTITUTIONS

OR "HOW CAN I ADD SOME VARIETY TO THE MENUS?"

BISCUIT MIX

We make our own biscuit mix to save money. This recipe makes three cups, but you can double, triple, etc.

Flour, enriched	2$^1/_4$ c
Baking Powder	4 T
Salt	$^1/_2$ t
Vegetable Shortening	$^1/_2$ c

1. Mix first three ingredients.
2. Cut in shortening (using a food processor for this saves time).
3. Store in covered container.

SPICE MIX

We make our own spice mix and use it instead of salt to flavor many of our recipes.

Onion Powder	$^1/_2$ c
Dried Parsley Flakes	$^3/_4$ c
Dried Oregano Leaves	3 T
Paprika	1 T
Garlic Powder	2 T
Basil Leaves	3 T

1. Make a shaker out of an empty glass jar by punching holes in the lid.
2. Mix all ingredients and pour mixture into the jar.
3. Use as needed.

SKILLET HOPPING JOHN

1 serving (about $^2/_3$ c) = 1 meat; 1 bread

	6	20	50	100
Onion, large whole	$^1/_2$	2	6	12
Garlic Cloves	1	2	3	6
Margarine	1 T	3 T	$^1/_2$ c	1 c
Black-eyed Peas, canned	$1^1/_2$–16 oz cans	5–16 oz cans	1–#10 + 5–16 oz cans	3–#10 + 4–16 oz cans
Chicken Rice Soup($10^1/_2$ oz can)	$^1/_2$ can	2 cans	5 cans	10 cans
Water	2 oz	4 oz	6 oz	12 oz
Brown Rice, uncooked	$^1/_2$ c	$1^1/_2$ c	$3^1/_2$ c	7 c
Garlic Powder	dash	1 t	1 T	2 T
Pimentos, chopped (optional)	Plenty, to taste			
Crushed Red Pepper (optional)	To taste			

1. Chop onion and garlic.
2. In iron skillet large enough to hold all ingredients, saute onion and garlic in margarine until onion is tender.
3. Drain and rinse black-eyed peas and add to onion and garlic.
4. Add remaining ingredients and bring mixture to a boil.
5. Cover. Turn heat down and simmer for 45-50 minutes.
6. Adults may like pimentos and red pepper. Children often do not.

TURKEY BURRITOS

1 burrito = 1 meat; 1 bread
Bake: 15 minutes at 300°

	6	20	50	100
Ground Turkey	10 oz	2 lb	5 lb	10 lb
Chili Powder	1½ t	2 T	¼ c	½ c
Onion Powder	½ t	½ T	1½ T	3 T
Cumin	½ t	½ T	1½ T	3 T
Paprika	dash	¼ t	1 t	2 t
Tomato Juice	6 T	1½ c	3 c	6 c
Cheddar Cheese	3 oz	11 oz	1 lb 12 oz	3 lb 8 oz
Flour Tortillas (6 inch)	6	20	50	100

1. Brown ground turkey in iron skillet.
2. Add spices and juice and mix well.
3. Simmer 15 minutes uncovered.
4. Wrap stack(s) of tortillas tightly in aluminum foil.
5. Heat wrapped tortillas in oven for 15 minutes at 300 degrees.
6. Spread equal amounts of meat mixture near one edge of warmed tortillas.
7. Shred cheese and sprinkle ⅛ cup cheese on each tortilla.
8. Fold edge over to cover filling.
9. Fold one side over envelope-style and roll tortilla, wrapping filling inside.
10. Place burritos in baking pan.
11. Cover tightly and keep in warm oven until cheese is melted or you are ready to serve.

SPAGHETTI SAUCE WITH TURKEY

1 serving = ½ meat; ½ fruit/vegetable

	12	20	50	100
Onion	⅓ c	⅔ c	1⅓ c	2⅔ c
Ground Turkey	1 lb	2 lb	4 lb	8 lb
Garlic Powder	1 T	2 T	4 T	8 T
Tomato Paste	6 oz can	12 oz	24 oz	48 oz
Stewed Tomatoes	1–28 oz can	2–28 oz cans	1–#10 + 1–16 oz can	2–#10 + 1–28 oz can
Basil	½ t	1 t	2 t	4 t
Oregano	½ t	1 t	2 t	4 t
Bay Leaf	1	1	2	4
Red Pepper	½ t	1 t	½ T	1 T

1. Chop onions in food processor.
2. Brown onions and turkey together in iron skillet. Be sure to break turkey into small pieces.
3. Add remainder of ingredients. Do not drain tomatoes.
4. Simmer 1-2 hours.

Note: Freezes well. For 6 servings, make 12 servings and freeze half for later use.

BISCUITS WITH WHEAT GERM

1 biscuit = 1 bread
Bake: 10-12 minutes at 450°

	20	50	100
Biscuit Mix (p. 142)	1¾ c	4¼ c	8½ c
Wheat Germ	½ c	1¼ c	2½ c
Sugar	1 T	2½ T	¼ c
Milk	¾ c	2 c	4 c

1. Mix dry ingredients.
2. Add milk and stir until dry ingredients are moistened.
3. Turn dough out onto a well-floured surface and knead 5 or 6 times.
4. Roll out to ½" thickness; cut with 2" biscuit cutter.
5. Place on cookie sheet coated with cooking spray.
6. Bake at 450 degrees for 10-12 minutes or until golden brown.
7. Freezes well.

CHEESE GRITS

1 serving = 1 bread
Bake: about an hour at 325°

	6	20	50	100
Grits, quick or regular, dry	½ c	1¼ c	1 lb 4 oz	2 lb 5 oz
Water	2 c	5 c	3 qt + 1⅓ c	1½ gal + 1⅓ c
Worcestershire Sauce	¾ t	2½ t	2 T + ¼ t	4 T + ½ t
Milk	¼ c	¾ c + 1 T	2¾ c	1 qt + 1⅓ c
Margarine	¾ t	2½ t	2 T + ¼ t	4 T + ½ t
Cheddar Cheese	2 oz	7 oz	1 lb	2 lb
Garlic Powder (optional)	½ t	½ T	1½ T	3 T
Eggs, medium	1	1	2	4
Paprika	dash	1 t	1 T	2 T

1. Cook grits until thick, according to directions on package. Omit salt.
2. Grate cheese.
3. Pour cooked grits into large mixing bowl and mix in Worcestershire, milk, margarine, garlic powder, and ½ the cheese.
4. Beat eggs and add to mixture.
5. Pour mixture into baking dish coated with cooking spray and sprinkle with remaining cheese and paprika.
6. Bake one hour or until lightly browned at 325 degrees.

CHICKEN FRIED RICE

1 serving = 1 bread; 1 meat

	6	20	50	100
Chicken, whole, uncooked	1 lb 10 oz	5 lb 4 oz	13 lb	26 lb 2 oz
Rice, converted, enriched	½ c	1½ c	3½ c	7 c
Oil	2 t	2 T	¼ c	½ c
Onion powder	½ t	½ T	1½ T	3 T
Garlic Powder	½ t	½ T	1½ T	3 T
Soy Sauce	1½ T	⅜ c	1 c	2 c
Eggs, medium	1	3	7	14

1. Place chicken in large soup pot and cover with water. Cover pan and bring to a boil. Lower heat and simmer chicken for 2 hours. Pour broth off chicken, reserving for use in making bouillon.
2. Remove chicken from bones and discard skin. Dice or shred chicken.
3. Cook rice according to instructions on package, but do not use salt. (Cook rice the day before for best results.)
3. Heat oil on medium heat.
4. When oil is hot, saute rice until slightly brown.
5. Add seasonings and stir until well mixed.
6. Make hole in middle of rice.
7. Beat eggs and pour into middle of rice.
8. Stir eggs constantly and as they cook, stir gradually into rice.
9. Add chicken and cook until eggs are done and mixture is heated through.

Note: Cook chicken and rice a day ahead to simplify preparation.

PASTA SALAD

1 serving = ½ meat; 1 bread

	6	20	50	100
Spice Mix (p. 142)	½ t	1¼ t	1 T + ⅛ t	2 T + ¼ t
Plain Yogurt	½ c	1¾ c	1 qt + ¼ c	2 qt + ⅓ c
Cottage Cheese	½ c	1¾ c	1 qt + ¼ c	2 qt + ⅓ c
Vinegar	¾ t	2½ t	2 T + ¼ c	¼ c + ½ t
Dill Weed	⅛ t	½ t	1 t	2 t
Spiral Pasta	3 oz	10 oz	1 lb 10 oz	3 lb 2 oz
Tuna	1–6½ oz can	3–6½ oz cans	¾–66½-oz can	1½–66½ oz cans

1. Puree all ingredients *except noodles and tuna* in a blender to make dressing. Store in refrigerator.
2. Cook noodles according to directions on package, but do not use salt.
3. Drain noodles.
4. Toss noodles with tuna until well blended.
5. Add dressing and chill overnight or at least 2 hours.

Note: The dressing for this salad is a good basic dressing for many pasta salads.

LIMA BEAN DELIGHT

1 serving = ½ fruit/vegetable
Bake: 45 minutes at 350°

	6	20	50	100
Bacon Slices	1	2	5	10
Margarine	1 T	3 T	½ c	1 c
Onion, chopped	2 T	⅓ c	1 c	2 c
Baby Lima Beans, frozen	½ lb	1 lb 4 oz	2 lb 8 oz	5 lb
Tomatoes, canned	½–16 oz can	16 oz can	2–28 oz cans	1–#10 can
Brown Sugar, packed	2 T	⅓ c	1 c	2 c
Chili Powder	⅛ t	½ t	1½ t	1 T
Vinegar	½ T	1½ T	¼ c	½ c

1. Cook bacon — drain fat, cool, and crumble.
1. Melt margarine in iron skillet over low heat.
2. Saute onions for 1 minute.
3. Combine ingredients (except bacon) in casserole coated with cooking spray.
4. Sprinkle crumbled bacon over top.
5. Bake at 350 degrees for 45 minutes.

STRAWBERRY MUFFINS

1 muffin = 1 bread

	24
Oil	1¼ c
Flour, whole wheat	1½ c
Flour, enriched	1½ c
Baking Soda	1 t
Salt	1 t
Cinnamon	3 t
Sugar	1½ c
Eggs, medium	3
Strawberries, frozen	2–10 oz packages
Colored Sugar Crystals (optional)	

1. Thaw strawberries. If strawberries have added sugar, decrease sugar in recipe by ½ cup.
2. Beat eggs.
3. Combine all ingredients and blend well.
4. Fill cupcake holders three-quarters full.
5. Bake at 350 degrees for 25 minutes (one hour if baking in loaf pans).
6. Decorate with colored sugar crystals (optional).

Note: This recipe also makes two 9x5x3 inch loaves of strawberry bread, but the Edwards girls like the bread so much we make "cupcakes" and decorate them with colored sugar for parties.

BEAN AND BEEF CASSEROLE

¾ c serving = 1 meat; 1 bread
Bake: 20 minutes at 325°

	12	20	50	100
Onion, large whole	½	1	2	4
Ground Beef	8 oz	1 lb	2 lb 8 oz	5 lb
Elbow Macaroni, enriched, dry	3 oz	8½ oz	1 lb 5 oz	2 lb 10 oz
Kidney Beans	1–16 oz can	2–16 oz cans	4–16 oz cans	1–#10 can
Oregano	1 T	2 T	¼ c	½ c
Tomato Sauce	1–15 oz can	2–15 oz cans	4–15 oz cans	1–#10 + 1–15 oz can
Cheddar Cheese	2 oz	4 oz	10 oz	1¼ lb
Mozzarella Cheese	2 oz	4 oz	10 oz	1¼ lb

1. Chop onion.
2. Combine onion and ground beef in iron skillet. Cook over medium heat until meat is browned.
3. Cook macaroni and drain.
4. Drain liquid from kidney beans and rinse.
5. Combine all ingredients, except cheeses, and pour into baking dish coated with cooking spray.
6. Shred cheeses and sprinkle on top of casserole.
7. Bake at 325 degrees until bubbly (about 20 minutes).
8. Freezes well.

CHICKEN CHOP SUEY

1 serving = 1 meat

	20	50	100
Chicken, whole	5 lb 5 oz	13 lb 4 oz	26 lb 7 oz
Celery, thinly sliced	¾ c	1⅔ c	3⅓ c
Onion, chopped	¼ c	⅔ c	1⅓ c
Oil	¼ c	⅔ c	1⅓ c
Cornstarch	1½ T	¼ c	½ c
Water	1 c	2½ c	5 c
Chicken Bouillon, cubes	1	3	5
Soy Sauce	⅓ c	1 c	2 c
Bean Sprouts, 16-oz can	1	2	4

1. Place chicken in large soup pot and cover with water. Cover pan and bring to a boil. Lower heat and simmer chicken for 2 hours. Pour broth off chicken, reserving for use in making bouillon.
2. Remove chicken from bones and discard skin. Dice or shred chicken.
3. Cook celery and onion in hot oil in skillet for about 2 minutes.
4. Blend cornstarch with water (chicken stock, if available) and stir into celery and onions.
5. Add chicken bouillon cubes and soy sauce.
6. Cook, stirring constantly, until sauce is thick and clear.
7. Drain and rinse bean sprouts and add to sauce.
8. Add cooked chicken.
9. Heat through and serve over rice or chow mein noodles. (Chow mein noodles are good but contain more fat.)

Note: Freezes well. If you are serving fewer than 20, freeze leftovers for later use.

FRUIT MOLD

1 serving = $^1/_2$ fruit/vegetable

	12	20	50	100
Orange Juice	¾ c	1¼ c	3 c + 1 T	1½ qt + 2 T
Gelatin	1 T	1 T + 2 t	¼ c + ½ t	½ c + 1 t
Pineapple Juice	¾ c	1¼ c	3 c + 1 T	1½ qt + 2 T
Lemon Juice	1 t	1½ t	1 T + 1 t	2 T + 2 t
Food Coloring				
Grapes, seedless	¾ c	1¼ c	1¼ lb	2½ lb
Crushed Pineapple, canned	1–8 oz can	2–8 oz cans	1½–20 oz cans	2¾–20 oz cans
Cottage Cheese (optional)	1 c	1⅔ c	1 qt + ¼ c	2 qt + ⅓ c

1. Chop grapes in food processor.
2. Drain and save juice.
3. Dissolve gelatin in orange juice and then boil gelatin mixture.
4. Add pineapple, lemon, and grape juices and food coloring to gelatin mixture and stir well.
5. Chill until thick but not set.
6. Add grapes and undrained pineapple to gelatin. Add cottage cheese, if desired.
7. Chill overnight or until set.

Note: Instead of 6 servings, make for 12 and serve twice in same week.

FRIENDSHIP STEW

1 serving = 1 meat; ½ fruit/vegetable

	20
Potatoes, medium	2
Carrots	2
Onions, medium	½
Celery	2 stalks
Ground Beef	3 lb
Beef Bouillon, granules	1 T
Spice Mix (page 142)	1 T
Tomatoes, canned	1–14½ oz can
Water	1–14½ oz can

1. Brown ground beef in iron skillet. Drain fat.
2. Dice potatoes and slice carrots, onions, and celery.
3. Put all in a pot. Add bouillon, spice mix, tomatoes, and water.
4. Cook uncovered for 1½ to 2 hours over low heat.

Note: Have each child bring in an ingredient for stew. Children can wash the vegetables and participate in the slicing, peeling, and chopping. Ask them to take a small taste of every ingredient before the stew is cooked. Other vegetables could also be used.

Alternatively, you could have the children play "Stone Soup." Start with a clean rock (large enough not to be swallowed!) and add vegetables according to the story.

FRUITY COLESLAW

1 serving ($^1/_4$ c) = $^1/_2$ fruit/vegetable

	6	20	50	100
Cabbage, whole	4 oz	13 oz	2 lb	4 lb
Carrots, whole	¼	1	2	4
Crushed Pineapple, canned	¼ c	⅔ c	2–8 oz cans	4–8 oz cans
Raisins	2 t	2½ T	⅜ c	¾ c
Mayonnaise, low-fat	2 T	½ c	1 c	2 c

1. Shred cabbage and carrots.
2. Drain pineapple.
3. Combine first four ingredients and chill.
4. Add mayonnaise, mix well, and serve.

COLE SLAW

1 serving = $1/2$ fruit/vegetable

	6	20	50	100
Sugar	2 T	¼ c + 2 T + 2 t	1 c + 2 t	2 c + 4 t
Vinegar	2 T	¼ c + 2 T + 2 t	1 c + 2 t	2 c + 4 t
Mayonnaise	3 T	½ c + 2 T	1½ c + 1 T	3 c + 2 T
Cabbage, whole	4 oz	13 oz	2 lb	4 lb

1. Combine first three ingredients in blender.
2. Refrigerate.
3. Shred cabbage and mix with dressing just before serving.

CARROT AND RAISIN MUFFINS

1 muffin = 1 bread
Bake: 15-20 minutes at 350°

	6	20	50
Flour, enriched	½ c	1⅔ c	4¼ c
Flour, whole wheat	½ c	1⅔ c	4¼ c
Baking Powder	1 t	3½ t	3 T
Pumpkin Pie Spice	⅛ t	½ t	1 T
Carrots, shredded	⅓ c	1 c + 2 T	2½ c
Raisins	¼ c	¾ c	1½ c
Eggs, medium	1	3	7
Milk	½ c	1⅔ c	1 qt + ¼ c
Oil	1 T	¼ c	⅔ c
Honey	2 T	½ c	1⅓ c

1. Combine first four ingredients.
2. Stir in carrots and raisins.
3. Combine egg, milk, oil, and honey and stir well. Combine with dry ingredients until just moistened.
4. Scoop into muffin tins coated with cooking spray.
5. Bake 15-20 minutes at 350 degrees.

Note: For 100 servings, make 2 batches of 50 to ensure light muffins.

SPINACH LASAGNA

1 serving = 1 bread; ½ fruit/vegetable; ½ meat
Bake: 55 minutes at 350°

	20	50	100
Lasagna	11 noodles	1½ lb.	3 lb
Spinach, chopped frozen,	2–10 oz pkgs	3 lb 12 oz	7 lb 8 oz
or fresh, trimmed	1 lb 5 oz	3 lb 5 oz	6 lb 10 oz
Cottage Cheese	1½ c	3¾ c	7½ c
Parmesan Cheese, grated	¼ c	⅔ c	1⅓ c
Nutmeg	1 t	2½ t	1½ t
Eggs, large	2	5	10
Tomato Sauce	2–15 oz cans	5–15 oz cans	1–#10 can + 1–15 oz can
Onion Powder	2 t	1½ T	3 T
Garlic Powder	2 t	1½ T	3 T
Oregano	2 t	1½ T	3 T
Cooking Spray			
Mozzarella Cheese, shredded	6 oz	1 lb	2 lb

1. Cook lasagna noodles according to package directions. Drain.
2. Thaw and drain spinach, if using frozen; chop, if using fresh.
3. Combine spinach, cottage cheese, Parmesan, nutmeg, and eggs, and mix well.
4. In separate container, mix tomato sauce, onion powder, garlic powder, and oregano.
5. Spray baking dish with cooking spray.

(continued on next page)

6. Starting with a thin layer of tomato sauce on bottom of pan, arrange a layer of noodles evenly over sauce. Top noodles with ⅓ of cheese mixture, sprinkle with ⅓ of mozzarella, spread on tomato sauce. Repeat layers, ending with sauce.
7. Cover pan with foil. Bake at 350 degrees for 40 minutes.
8. Remove foil and bake 15 minutes more.

Note: Remember to keep your conversation positive if children ask "What's this green stuff?" Talk about spinach (even mention Popeye and sing his theme song!) and give the recipe a chance. Don't give up after the first try!

Lasagna freezes well. If serving fewer than 20, freeze extra lasagna to be served later.

TOMATO RICE

1 serving = 1 bread; ½ fruit/vegetable
Bake: 20 minutes at 350°

	6	20	50	100
Onions	2 T	1 small	1 medium	1 large
Garlic	½ clove	2 cloves	5 cloves	10 cloves
Parsley	1 t	1 T	2½ T	5 T
Olive Oil	1 t	1 T	2½ T	5 T
Tomatoes, canned	1–16 oz can	2–28 oz cans	1–#10 can	2–#10 cans
Rice, converted, enriched, dry	½ c	1½ c	3½ c	7 c
Tomato Paste	1 t	1 T	2½ T	5 T
Cooking Spray				
Parmesan Cheese	2 T	½ c	1¼ c	2½ c

1. Chop onions, garlic, and parsley in food processor.
2. Heat oil in iron skillet over medium heat and add onions, garlic, and parsley. Heat for 2 minutes.
3. Chop tomatoes with liquid in food processor and add to onions. Heat for 3 minutes.
4. Stir in rice and tomato paste.
5. Place in baking dish sprayed with cooking spray and cover; bake at 350 degrees for 15 minutes or until rice is tender.
6. Stir in Parmesan and bake 5 minutes more.

Note: May substitute ketchup for tomato paste in small quantities.

LOW-SUGAR "CUT-OUT" COOKIES

Bake: 8-10 minutes at 350°

	60
Margarine	1 c
Sugar	1 c
Baking Soda	½ t
Milk	2 T
Eggs	2
Flavoring (vanilla, almond, your choice)	1 t
Flour	4 c

1. Cream margarine and sugar.
2. Dissolve baking soda in milk.
3. Add soda/milk, eggs, and flavoring. Mix well.
4. Add flour, one cup at a time, mixing well after each addition. Dough will be very stiff.
5. Chill dough 2 hours.
6. Roll out and cut shapes as desired.
7. Bake at 350 degrees for 8 to 10 minutes.

CHAPTER TEN

PARTY CELEBRATIONS

OR "SHOULD I SPEND $14 FOR A BIRTHDAY CAKE FROSTED WITH SHORTENING AND POWDERED SUGAR?"

It is important to be consistent about what you feed children. Parties should not be a time when anything goes, especially when you consider that a child might be included in several parties in one week.

Children can have fun at a party, even if cake is not served. The most important thing is that the birthday person feel special. Candles in banana bread or bran muffins signify that this snack is special. It is someone's birthday!

In the interest of healthy teeth and good nutrition, we suggest candy and other sugar treats not be included in celebrations. At the very least, keep sugar treats to a minimum and encourage children to brush their teeth following the party. All of our party recipes are designed to be moderate in fat, salt, and sugar, while still being festive.

Homemade baked goods that have no more than a 1:3 ratio of sugar to flour are delicious and have half the sugar that is sometimes called for in recipes. (Check your state regulations before serving homemade treats. Some states don't allow homemade food in child care settings.) Also, children do not seem to like icing very much and many icings contain more sugar than neces-sary for taste. However, children do enjoy colorful baked goods and decorating a cake with sprinkles or using tube icing is a fun and harmless way to increase the appeal of a party treat.

You can have more control over party foods if you make them yourself or provide guidelines for parents. Figure 10-1 shows a sample letter, including a list of party do's and don'ts, which can be sent to the parent just prior to the child's birthday. A letter like this can encourage parent cooperation and help to ensure the success of your party policy.

Party menus should meet snack requirements if served during snack and claimed for reimbursement. Since cake is not reimbursable, even if it is homemade, snack requirements must be met with other items. Our party menus include foods which are reimbursable.

Celebrating the cultural holidays of the children in your home or center will develop an appreciation for cultural diversity in children and create opportunities for fun and learning. A good reference for information about holidays of different cultures is *Resources for Creative Teaching in Early Childhood Education* by Bonnie Mack Flemming and Darlene Softley Hamilton (Harcourt, Brace, Jovanovich).

Figure 10-1
Sample Party Letter

Dear _____:

Your child _____ has a birthday coming up next week! The children love birthdays. If you are planning to have a birthday party here, please familiarize yourself with the Birthday Party Guidelines provided below.

All of the meals provided by _____ are moderate in fat, salt, and sugar. We feel it is important to be consistent about what we feed children and not completely ignore those guidelines even at party time. This is especially important when you consider that your child might be included in several parties in one week when birthdays cluster in the same month.

Also, we have learned that children do not necessarily like icing very much, and many icings contain more sugar than necessary for taste. Children like colorful baked goods and you can decorate a cake with sprinkles or use tube icing to write names or small decorations on cakes or cookies, and keep the amount of sugar to a minimum.

We have learned too, that fancy cakes and elaborate parties encourage competitiveness among children for the "best" party, and take some of the joy and pleasure from the celebration. For this reason, we ask that you not provide individual party favors for the children in the class.

If your child wants to give something to the whole class, consider donating a book or a new toy to the classroom. Party decorations that we do find to be fun are decorative plates, napkins, and/or hats. Please don't send noisemakers, chewing gum, or candy for the party.

A summary of Party Do's and Don'ts is listed below:

Party Do's

Homemade cakes, breads, cookies using no more than 1 part sugar to 2 parts flour*

Cake icings or decorations with little sugar

Low-fat frozen yogurt

100% fruit juice or fresh fruits

Gift to the class (if desired)

Decorative plates, napkins, and/or hats

Party Don'ts

Bakery, grocery, or box mix cakes, cookies, and breads

Anything chocolate

Ice cream

Powdered drink mixes, fruit punch that is not 100% fruit juice

Individual party favors

Noisemakers, chewing gum, and candy

We would be glad to share recipes which adhere to the Birthday Party Guidelines. Feel free to ask about these. If you prefer, you may order a cake or baked item three days in advance from our cook. We appreciate your cooperation in this matter. We know your child is going to have a very HAPPY BIRTHDAY!

Sincerely yours,

*Note: Some states have regulations forbidding homemade food in some types of programs. Check with your licenser for the rule in your state.

PARTY MENUS

SNACK	SERVING SIZE=REQUIREMENT
Melon Boat	½ c = 1 fruit
Cupcake Paper Pickups	8 crackers = 1 bread
100% Fruit Juice Punch (optional)	
PBY Flip	½ c = 1 meat; ½ fruit
Party Pancake	2" square = 1 bread
Milk, fluid	½ c = 1 milk
Fruit Syrup (optional)	
Bran Muffin	1 muffin = 1 bread
Pineapple/Banana Shake or Fruitshake	1 c = 1 fruit
Funny Fruit (optional)	
Strawberries	½ c = 1 fruit
Milk, fluid	½ c = 1 milk
Cake (optional)	
Frozen Yogurt Sandwiches	1 sandwich = 1 bread
Juice, 100% fruit	½ c = 1 fruit
Yogurt (optional)	

(continued on next page)

Banana Bread	1 slice = 1 bread
100% Fruit Juice Punch	½ c = 1 fruit

Potato Pancakes and Sour Cream	2 pancakes = ½ fruit/vegetable
Applesauce	¼ c = ½ fruit/vegetable
Milk	½ c = 1 milk

Party Ambrosia (1/2 recipe)	¼ c = 1 fruit/vegetable
Carrot/Raisin Muffin (mini muffin size)	1 muffin = ½ bread
Milk	½ c = 1 milk

RECIPES

100% FRUIT JUICE PUNCH

Equal parts orange juice and pineapple juice. See Quick Reference Chart (inside front cover, last page and inside back cover) for amount of juice needed. Add ice cubes made from cranberry juice.

PINEAPPLE/BANANA SHAKE

One serving (1 c) = 1 fruit

	6	20	50	100
Orange Juice	3/4 c	2-1/2 c	6 c	12-1/2 c
Pineapple Juice	3/4 c	2-1/2 c	6 c	12-1/2 c
Bananas	3	5	13	25
Milk	4-1/2 c	15 cups	1 qt + 5-1/2 c	4-1/2 gal + 3 c
Ice Cubes	3 cubes	10 cubes	25 cubes	50 cubes

1. Mix shake for 6-8 servings at a time — do NOT mix more.
2. Put all ingredients in a blender.
3. Blend on high.
4. Serve immediately or store shake in refrigerator to keep chilled.
5. If refrigerated, stir briskly before serving.

Note: Children enjoy drinking the shake with a straw.

FRUITSHAKE

1 serving (½ c) = 1 fruit/vegetable

	6	20	50	100
Bananas, large	2	6	15	30
Strawberries, sliced frozen	½ c	1½ c	4½ c (2 lb 9 oz)	9 c (5 lb 2 oz)
Orange Juice	1½ c	5½ c	13½ c (3 qt + 1½ c)	27 c (1½ gal + 3 c)

1. Mix all ingredients in blender until smooth.
2. Refrigerate until time to serve.

WATERMELON BOAT

1 serving (½ c) = 1 fruit/vegetable

Children think a bowl made from half a watermelon is really neat! You can put candles in holders and place them around the rim of the "bowl." See Quick Reference Chart (inside front cover, last page and inside back cover), to determine how much fruit you will need to purchase.

1. Cut watermelon in half.
2. Make melon balls out of the inside of one melon half. Cut decorative edges around scooped-out melon rind, if desired.
3. Fill melon shell with melon balls and other fruits in season.

FROZEN YOGURT SANDWICHES

1 serving (2 cookies) = 1 bread

1. Make enough lemon cookies (p. 125) for two per child.
2. Slice frozen yogurt lengthwise in ½" sections. (You can cut through the cardboard.)
3. Cut 2" rounds with biscuit cutter.
4. Place round of yogurt between two cookies.
5. Store in freezer with wax paper between layers.
6. Keep these on hand for last minute party fun.

CUPCAKE PAPER PICKUPS

1 serving (7 animal or 32 fish crackers) = 1 bread

Fill cupcake papers with animal crackers or "fish" crackers. Serve with fresh fruit. See Quick Reference Chart, inside front cover, last page and inside back cover, to determine how many crackers you need to purchase.

FUNNY FRUIT

1 serving = 1 fruit/vegetable

Serve each child one slice of pineapple and a canned peach half. Give them bowls of coconut, sesame seeds, and sprinkles and let them decorate their piece of fruit any way they like.

WHIPPED CREAM ICING

Whipping Cream, 1 c
Sugar, ½ T

1. Whip cream, adding sugar before cream is stiff.
2. Makes enough for one 9 x 13 inch cake.

CREAM CHEESE ICING

Cream Cheese, 8 oz
Confectioners Sugar or Honey, ¼ c
Whipping Cream (optional)
Food Coloring (optional)

1. Soften cream cheese.
2. Using a mixer, combine confectioners sugar or honey with cream cheese. Adding some whipped cream gives a lighter texture and allows for easier spreading.
3. If you like, add food coloring at the end.
4. Makes enough for one 9 x 13 inch cake.

PARTY PANCAKE

1 serving (one 6" pancake) = 1 bread

1. Make pancake batter using recipe on p. 134.
2. Grease cookie sheet with cooking spray.
3. Write a birthday message on the sheet with some batter. You can use a baster or a pastry tube, but be sure to form the mirror image of letters because this will be the top of the pancake. (You could also make a simple smiling face.)
4. Bake words for 5 minutes at 350 degrees.
5. Cover words with remainder of batter and bake for 15 minutes.
6. Remove from oven and turn out onto another cookie sheet or onto cardboard covered with foil.
7. Serve immediately with fruit juice syrup, if desired.

FRUIT JUICE SYRUP

	6	20	50	100
Corn Starch	2 T	4 T	½ c	1 c
Apple, Pineapple, or other light-flavored juice	1½ c	1 qt + 1 c	3 qt + ½ c	1½ gal + 1 c

1. Mix part of cold juice with corn starch — ¼ cup cold juice for every 2 tablespoons of corn starch.
2. Place remaining juice in sauce pan and heat over moderate heat until bubbly.
3. Add corn starch mixture, stirring constantly.
4. Keep stirring until thickened.
5. Remove from heat and serve.

BUTTERMILK CAKE

Bake: 30 minutes at 350°

Flour	3 c
Baking Powder	1½ t
Baking Soda	½ t
Margarine	⅔ c
Sugar	1¼ c
Eggs	3
Vanilla	2 t
Buttermilk	1 c
Cooking Spray	

1. Sift flour, baking powder, and baking soda together.
2. Cream margarine and sugar; beat until fluffy.
3. Separate eggs and mix yolks, one at a time, with margarine and sugar.
4. Add vanilla to buttermilk.
5. Add sifted dry ingredients alternately with buttermilk to creamed mixture, mixing just enough after each addition to keep batter smooth.
6. Beat egg whites until stiff.
7. Fold egg whites into batter.
8. Pour into 9 x 13 inch pan greased with cooking spray.
9. Bake for 30 minutes at 350 degrees.

TOMATO CAKE

Bake: 30-35 minutes at 350°

	6	20
Flour	1 c	2 c
Baking Soda	⅛ t	¼ t
Baking Powder	1½ t	3 t
Ground Cinnamon	¼ t	¾ t
Ground Cloves	¼ t	¾ t
Nutmeg	¼ t	¾ t
Vegetable Oil	⅓ c	¾ c
Sugar	⅓ c	¾ c
Eggs	1	2
Tomato Soup, condensed (10 ¾ oz)	½ can	1 can
Cooking Spray		
Pan	loaf	10 x 10 inch

1. Sift flour with baking soda, baking powder, and spices.
2. Thoroughly combine oil and sugar.
3. Add eggs to creamed mixture; beat until light and fluffy.
4. Add dry ingredients alternately with soup, mixing until smooth after each addition.
5. Pour into greased (with cooking spray) and floured pan.
6. Bake 30-35 minutes at 350 degrees.
7. Cool 10 minutes; remove from pan and cool on rack.

Note: The recipe for 20 makes 25 2 x 2 inch squares. You could make 2 cakes for 50 or 4 cakes for 100 children.

POTATO PANCAKE

1 serving (2 pancakes) = ½ fruit/vegetable

	6	20	50	100
Potatoes	¾ lb	2½ lb	6¼ lb	12½ lb
Margarine	1 T	¼ c	⅔ c	1⅓ c
Onion Powder	⅛ t	½ t	1¼ t	2½ t
Milk	1 T	¼ c	⅔ c	1⅓ c
Ginger	⅛ t	½ t	1¼ t	2½ t
Eggs, medium	1	3	7	14
Oil				

1. Boil and mash potatoes.
2. Add remaining ingredients. Mix well and set aside to cool.
3. Dust hands with flour.
4. Using ⅛ c scoop, shape dough into pancakes.
5. Lightly oil iron skillet.
6. Cook pancakes over medium heat until brown on both sides.

Note: Potato pancakes are a variation of latkes which are served at Hanukkah. They are delicious served with applesauce as a breakfast or party treat.

Cook extra potatoes for this recipe when you prepare mashed potatoes. You can make the pancake dough one day, refrigerate it overnight, and prepare the pancakes the next day.

PARTY AMBROSIA

1 serving = 1 fruit

	6	20	50	100
Mandarin Oranges, canned	1 lb can	3–1 lb cans	7–1 lb cans	14–1 lb cans
Miniature Marshmallows	¼ c	¾ c	1¾ c	3½ c
Purple Grapes, seedless	12 oz	2 lb 10 oz	5 lb 12 oz	11 lb 8 oz

1. Chop grapes in food processor and drain. (Chop to prevent choking hazard.)
2. Place chopped grapes in a bowl and add remaining ingredients.
3. Mix well.
4. Refrigerate until time to serve.

PBY FLIP

One serving (½ c) = 1 meat; ½ fruit/vegetable

	6	20	50	100
Bananas	3	10	25	50
Vanilla or Lemon Yogurt	¾ c	2½ c	6¼ c	12½ c
Peanut Butter, creamy	¾ c	2½ c	6¼ c	12½ c

1. Put all ingredients in a blender.
2. Blend until smooth.
3. Place in individual five ounce cups.
4. Chill thoroughly before serving.

Note: This recipe works best when you make servings for 6 at a time. Other quantities are given to show ingredient amounts necessary for number of servings.

APPENDICES

Appendix A - Cooking Miscellany

SCOOPS

You might use scoops for portioning such foods as drop cookies, muffins, meat patties, casseroles, and some vegetables and salads. The number on the scoop shows the number of scoops that make one quart. The following table shows the approximate measure of each scoop in cups, tablespoons, and teaspoons.

Scoop Number	Level Measure
6	⅔ cup
8	½ cup
10	⅜ cup
12	⅓ cup
16	¼ cup
20	3⅕ tablespoons
24	2⅔ tablespoons
30	2⅕ tablespoons
40	1⅗ tablespoons
50	3⅘ teaspoons
60	1 tablespoon

LADLES

You may use ladles to serve soups, stews, creamed dishes, sauces, gravies, and other similar food. The following sizes of ladles are most frequently used. Although the ladles are labeled "ounce," they are actually "fluid ounce" which is a volume, not a weight measurement.

Number on Ladle	Approximate Measure
1 ounce	⅛ cup
2 ounce	¼ cup
4 ounce	½ cup
6 ounce	¾ cup
8 ounce	1 cup

CONVERSION CHART

Follow these steps to convert a recipe to one which will serve more or fewer people.

1. Determine the number of servings needed and the yield of the selected recipe.
2. Divide the number of servings needed by the yield amount. This will determine the factor. The factor will be greater than 1.0 when increasing the number of servings and less than 1.0 when decreasing the number of servings.
3. Multiply the amount of each ingredient by the factor to obtain the amount needed for the desired number of servings.
4. Change any decimal parts to the nearest measurable amounts, i.e., 6½ eggs would become 7 eggs.

A conversion chart for recipes written for 50 servings is provided below. Multiply the ingredient quantities for 50 servings by the factor shown for the number of servings desired.

Number of Servings	Factor
5	.1
10	.2
15	.3
20	.4
25	.5

Number of Servings	Factor
30	.6
35	.7
40	.8
45	.9
50	1.0
55	1.1
60	1.2
65	1.3
70	1.4
75	1.5
80	1.6
85	1.7
90	1.8
95	1.9
100	2.0

For amounts over 100, add the factor for 100 to the factor for the amount over 100.

$$135 \text{ servings} = \begin{array}{rr} 100 & 2.0 \\ +35 & \underline{.7} \\ & 2.7 \end{array}$$

Remember to change any decimal parts of ingredients to the nearest measurable amounts.

Ramona DeBoer at the Tennessee CACFP office provided the following recipe conversion example:

BAKED CUSTARD

Ingredients	50 servings	x	Factor		For 25 servings
Eggs	13 large	x	.5	=	7
Sugar	1-1/3 cups	x	.5	=	3/4 cup
Salt	1/2 teaspoon	x	.5	=	1/4 teaspoon
Vanilla	1 tablespoon	x	.5	=	1-1/2 teaspoon
Hot Milk	2-1/4 quarts	x	.5	=	1 quart+1/2 cup
Nutmeg	1 teaspoon	x	.5	=	1/2 teaspoon

Equivalent Common Food Measures

1 tablespoon	=	3 teaspoons
1 fluid ounce	=	2 tablespoons
1/8 cup	=	2 tablespoons
1/4 cup	=	4 tablespoons
1/3 cup	=	5-1/3 tablespoons
1/2 cup	=	8 tablespoons
2/3 cup	=	10-2/3 tablespoons
3/4 cup	=	12 tablespoons
1 cup	=	16 tablespoons
1 pint	=	2 cups
1 quart	=	2 pints
1 gallon	=	4 quarts
1 peck	=	8 quarts
1 bushel	=	4 pecks

Changing ounces to pounds

1 ounce	=	.062 pound
2 ounces	=	.125 pound
3 ounces	=	.187 pound
4 ounces	=	.250 pound
5 ounces	=	.312 pound
6 ounces	=	.375 pound
7 ounces	=	.438 pound
8 ounces	=	.500 pound
9 ounces	=	.562 pound
10 ounces	=	.625 pound
11 ounces	=	.688 pound
12 ounces	=	.750 pound
13 ounces	=	.812 pound
14 ounces	=	.875 pound
15 ounces	=	.938 pound
16 ounces	=	1.000 pound

RECOMMENDED UTENSILS

You should invest in cast iron skillets for cooking meats. Many people have given up their iron skillets for non-stick coated or stainless steel skillets. The food you are preparing picks up valuable iron from the skillet. See p. 20.

Invest in a vegetable steamer to avoid nutrient loss when preparing vegetables.

Buy a candy thermometer and an oven thermometer. The candy thermometer is invaluable when it comes to baking recipes containing yeast. The oven thermometer will help you gauge your oven's temperature which frequently does not match the temperature control.

A variety of pan sizes and types are necessary. Stainless steel is both durable and unbreakable.

Clear plastic measuring cups make measuring a little easier and they will not shatter if you drop them.

One of the biggest investments but most worthwhile is a scale that will weigh foods up to 10 pounds in 1 ounce increments. It is much easier for kitchens which prepare for large groups to weigh food rather than measure it by volume. A good example of this is weighing macaroni or spaghetti. Even small kitchens would benefit from a scale.

COMMON CAN AND JAR SIZES

Can Size (industy term)[1]	Average net weight of fluid measure per can[2]		Average volume per can		Cans per case	Principal products
	Customary	Metric	Cups	Liters	Number	
# 10	6 lb (96 oz) to 7 lb 5 oz (117 oz)	2.72 kg to 3.31 kg	12 to 13⅔	2.84 to 3.24	6	Institutional size: Fruits, vegetables, some other foods.
# 3 Cyl	51 oz (3 lb 3 oz) or 46 fl oz (1 qt 14 fl oz)	1.44 kg or 1.36 L	5¾	1.36	12	Condensed soups, some vegetables, meat and poultry products, fruit and vegetable juices.
# 2½	26 oz (1 lb 10 oz) to 30 oz (1 lb 14 oz)	737 g to 850 g	3½	0.83	24	Family size: Fruits, some vegetables.
# 2 Cyl	24 fl oz	709 mL	3	0.71	24	Juices, soups.
# 2	20 oz (1 lb 4 oz) or 18 fl oz (1 pt 2 fl oz)	567 g or 532 mL	2½	0.59	24	Juices, ready-to-serve soups, some fruits.

Can Size (industy term)[1]	Average net weight of fluid measure per can[2]		Average volume per can		Cans per case	Principal products
	Customary	Metric	Cups	Liters	Number	
# 303	16 oz (1 lb) to 17 oz (1 lb 1 oz)	453 g to 481 g	2	0.47	24 or 36	Small cans: Fruits and vegetables, some meat and poultry products, ready-to-serve soups.
# 300	14 oz to 16 oz (1 lb)	396 g to 453 g	1¾	0.41	24	Some fruits and meat products.
# 2 (vacuum)	12 oz	340 g	1½	0.36	24	Principally vacuum pack corn.
# 1 (picnic)	10½ oz to 12 oz	297 g to 340 g	1¼	0.30	48	Condensed soups, some fruits, vegetables, meat, fish.
8 oz	8 oz	226 g	1	0.24	48 or 72	Ready-to-serve soups, fruits, vegetables.

[1]Can sizes are industry terms and do not necessarily appear on the label.
[2]The net weight on can or jar labels differs according to the density of the contents. For example: A # 10 can of cranberry sauce weighs 7 lb 5 oz (3.32 kg). Meats, fish, and shellfish are known and sold by weight of contents.

Appendix B - Food and Nutrition Service Regional Offices

New England Regional Office
Burlington, MA
Connecticut, Maine, Massachusetts, New Hampshire, Rhode Island, Vermont

Mid-Atlantic Regional Office
Robbinsville, NJ
Delaware, Maryland, New Jersey, New York, Pennsylvania, Washington, D.C., Virginia, West Virginia, Puerto Rico, Virgin Islands

Southeast Regional Office
Atlanta, GA
Alabama, Florida, Georgia, Kentucky, Mississippi, North Carolina, South Carolina, Tennessee

Midwest Regional Office
Chicago, Illinois
Illinois, Indiana, Michigan, Minnesota, Ohio, Wisconsin

Mountain Plains Regional Office
Denver, Colorado
Colorado, Iowa, Kansas, Missouri, Montana, Nebraska, North Dakota, South Dakota, Utah, Wyoming

Southwest Regional Office
Dallas, Texas
Arkansas, Louisiana, New Mexico, Oklahoma, Texas

Western Regional Office
San Francisco, California
Alaska, American Samoa, Arizona, California, Guam, Hawaii, Idaho, Nevada, Oregon, Trust Territory of the Pacific Islands, Commonwealth of the Northern Mariana Islands, Washington

NOTES

CHAPTER ONE

[1] American Academy of Pediatrics Committee on Nutrition, "Prudent Life-style for Children: Dietary Fat and Cholesterol," Pediatrics 78 No. (3) (September 1986), p. 524.

[2] LaRosa and Finberg, "Preliminary report from a conference entitled 'Prevention of Adult Atherosclerosis During Childhood'," Journal of Pediatrics, 112 (February 1988), p. 317.

[3] American Heart Association, The American Heart Association Diet — An Eating Plan for Healthy Americans (Dallas: 1985).

[4] U.S. Department of Health and Human Services, The Surgeon General's Report on Nutrition and Health (Washington, D.C.: GPO, 1988), p.12.

[5] American Academy of Pediatrics Committee on Nutrition, "Plant Fiber Intake in the Pediatric Diet," Pediatrics 67 No. (4) (April, 1981), pp. 572-575.

[6] American Dental Association, Diet and Dental Health (Chicago: 1990) p. 6.

[7] American Heart Association Diet.

[8] Diet and Dental Health, pp. 6-7.

[9] U.S. Department of Agriculture and U.S. Department of Health and Human Services, Nutrition and Your Health - Dietary Guidelines for Americans. Home and Garden Bulletin No. 232 (Washington, D.C.: GPO, 1985), p. 20.

[10] U.S. Department of Health and Human Services, Surgeon General's Report, p. 13.

[11] Whitney, Cataldo, Rolfes, Understanding Normal and Clinical Nutrition (St. Paul: West Publishing Company, 1987), p. 419.

CHAPTER THREE

[1] Schmitt, <u>Your Child's Health,</u> (New York: Bantam Books, 1987), p. 236.

[2] The American Dietetic Association, <u>Good Eaters — Not Tiny Tyrants: Feeding Children Ages 3-5,</u> (Chicago: 1986)

[3] Furman, "Please Eat!," <u>Baby Talk,</u> (July 1990), p. 39.

[4] Schmitt, p. 239.

[5] Pugliese et al., "Parental Health Beliefs as a Cause of Nonorganic Failure to Thrive," <u>Pediatrics</u> 80 No. (2) (August 1987), p. 181.

[6] Hare, "Calorie Needs of Children - How Much is Enough?," <u>Child Care Center,</u> (March 1988), p. 46.

[7] <u>Good Eaters</u>

[8] Schmitt, p. 239.

[9] Schmitt, pp. 239-240.

[10] <u>Good Eaters</u>

[11] Baker, O'Neill, Karpf, <u>The Injury Fact Book,</u> (Lexington, MA: Lexington Books, 1984), p. 167.

[12] American Academy of Pediatrics, <u>Choking Prevention and First Aid for Infants and Children,</u> (Chicago: 1988)

[13] Harris, et al., "Childhood Asphyxiation by Food," <u>Journal of the American Medical Association,</u> 251, (May 4, 1984), p. 2233-34.

[14] Baker, et al., p. 167.

[15] <u>Choking Prevention.</u>

CHAPTER FOUR

[1] U.S. Department of Agriculture Food and Nutrition Service, <u>Food Buying Guide for Child Nutrition Programs</u>, USDA-FNS Program Aid #1331. (January, 1984), p. 6.

HELPFUL TIPS

1. Soaking raisins in water pulls the sweetness from the raisins into the water, providing a natural sweetener when the raisin water is used for cooking. (See Oatmeal with Raisins, p. 105.)

2. When you make meatloaf consider doubling the recipe and freezing the extras. Also, salt is optional in our meatloaf recipe, p. 106. Make meatloaf without salt at first. If the children eat it well, you will have found a way to reduce the salt in their diet.

3. Use more bread than required when using peanut butter and chicken salad as sandwich spreads. Children might choke on ¼ cup of chicken salad, or 1½ tablespoons of peanut butter on a half of a sandwich. When serving Peanut Butter and Lettuce Sandwiches (p. 109) or Chicken Salad Sandwiches (p. 130), consider making open-faced sandwiches if you don't want to use two slices of bread to make whole sandwiches.

When using peanut butter as an optional spread on Raisin Toast (p. 101), use a whole piece of toast.

4. Potato chips are not a CACFP reimbursable food item, so the quantity to serve is up to you. We suggest you use unsalted potato chips or apple chips.

5. CACFP requires that yogurt be purchased from the dairy case. It may not be canned, homemade or frozen. Yogurt can be used as a meat alternate component of the Snack meal pattern, but it is not a reimbursable food for Breakfast or Lunch.

6. The quantities of fruit in the Quick Reference Chart are the minimum required amount of fruit, for all forms of fruit purchased. Fruit quantities were based on the lowest yield form of canned fruit and small fresh fruit sizes.

BIBLIOGRAPHY

American Academy of Pediatrics. <u>Choking Prevention and First Aid for Infants and Children.</u> Chicago: 1988.

American Academy of Pediatrics Committee on Nutrition. 1981. Plant fiber intake in the pediatric diet. <u>Pediatrics</u> 67 (4): 575.

American Academy of Pediatrics Committee on Nutrition. 1986. Prudent lifestyle for children: dietary fat and cholesterol. <u>Pediatrics</u> 78 (3): 524.

American Dental Association. <u>Diet and Dental Health.</u> Chicago: 1990.

American Dietetic Association. <u>Good Eaters – Not Tiny Tyrants: Feeding Children Ages 3-5.</u> Chicago: 1986.

American Heart Association. <u>Dietary Guidelines for Healthy American Adults.</u> Dallas: 1986.

American Heart Association. <u>The American Heart Association Diet - An Eating Plan for Healthy Americans.</u> Dallas: 1985.

Baker, Susan P., Brian O'Neill, and Ronald S. Karpf. <u>The Injury Fact Book.</u> Lexington, Massachusetts: Lexington Books, 1984.

Furman, Lydia. "Please Eat!" <u>Baby Talk</u>. July 1990: 39.

Hare, Karen L. "Calorie Needs of Children - How much is Enough?" <u>Child Care Center</u>. March 1988: 46.

Harris, Carole Stallings, Baker, Susan P.; Smith, Gary A.; and Harris, Richard M. 1984. "Childhood asphyxiation by food." <u>JAMA</u> 251 (17): 2233-2234.

Kowalski, Robert E. Cholesterol and Children. New York: Harper and Row, 1989.

LaRosa, John and Finberg, Lawrence. 1988. Preliminary report from conference entitled "Prevention of Adult Atherosclerosis During Childhood." J. Peds. 112 (2): 517.

Pugliese, Michael T.; Weyman-Daum, Michelle; Moses, Nancy; and Lifshitz, Fima. 1987. Parental health beliefs as a cause of nonorganic failure to thrive. Pediatrics. 80 (2): 181.

Schmitt, Barton. Your Child's Health. New York: Bantam Books, 1987.

U.S. Department of Agriculture Food and Nutrition Service. Food Buying Guide for Child Nutrition Programs. USDA-FNS Program Aid #1331. Washington, D.C.: 1984.

U.S. Department of Agriculture and U.S. Department of Health and Human Services. Nutrition and Your Health - Dietary Guidelines for Americans. Home and Garden Bulletin #232. Washington, D.C.: 1985.

U.S. Department of Health and Human Services. The Surgeon General's Report on Nutrition and Health. Washington, D.C.: 1988.

Whitney, Eleanor Noss, Corinne Balog Cataldo, Sharon Rady Rolfes. Understanding Normal and Clinical Nutrition. St. Paul: West Publishing, 1987.

Widome, Mark D. "First Aid for Choking." Healthy Kids. Vol. 1, No. 2 (1989) 26, 31-32.

INDEX

Other Publications From Redleaf Press

All the Colors We Are, Todos los Colores de Nuestra Piel-
Magnificent photos and simple, engaging language
capture the essence of how we get our skin coloring.
Includes unique activity ideas. Bilingual.

*Basic Guide To Family Child Care Record Keeping: Fourth
Edition* – Clear instructions on keeping necessary family
child care business records.

Busy Fingers, Growing Minds – Over 200 original and
traditional finger plays, with enriching activities for all
parts of a curriculum.

Calendar-Keeper – Activities, family child care record
keeping, recipes and more. Updated annually. Most
popular publication in the field.

Family Child Care Contracts and Policies – Sample contracts and policies, and how-to information on using
them effectively to improve your business.

Family Child Care Tax Workbook – Updated every year,
latest step-by-step information on filling out forms,
how to figure out depreciation, etc.

*Heart to Heart Caregiving: A Sourcebook of Family Day Care
Activities, Projects and Practical Provider Support* – Excellent ideas and guidance from an experienced provider.

*Practical Solutions to Practically Every Problem: The Early
Childhood Teacher's Manual* – Over 300 proven develop-
mentally appropriate solutions for all kinds of classroom
problems.

*Roots & Wings: Affirming Culture in Early Childhood
Programs* – A new approach to multicultural education
that helps shape positive attitudes toward cultural
differences.

Snail Trails and Tadpole Tails – A fun nature curriculum
with five easy-to-do, hands-on units that explore the
lifecycle of these intriguing creatures: snails, earth-
worms, frogs, praying mantises and silkworms.

*Those Mean Nasty Dirty Downright Disgusting but . . .
Invisible Germs* – A delightful story that reinforces for
children the benefits of frequent hand washing.

*Transition Magician: Strategies for Guiding Young Children
in Early Childhood Programs* – This first-of-a-kind book
helps you plan transition times. Lots of new ideas and
over 200 original learning activities.

CALL FOR CATALOG OR
ORDERING INFORMATION
1-800-423-8309

FOOD ITEM	SERVING SIZE for Children 3 through 5 years	PURCHASE AMOUNT FOR NUMBER OF SERVINGS			
		6	20	50	100
Rices, dry					
full requirement	¼ c cooked				
Brown or converted, enriched		½ c	1½ c	3½ c	7 c
Rice cakes, enriched ½ requirement	1½ cakes	9 cakes	30 cakes	75 cakes	150 cakes
FRUITS					
Canned (Applesauce, apples, fruit cocktail, mandarin oranges, peaches, pears, pineapple)					
full requirement	½ c	24 oz	6–1 lb cans	2–#10 cans	4–#10 cans
½ requirement	¼ c	1½ c	3–1 lb cans	1–#10 cans	2–#10 cans
Fresh Apples, Bananas, Oranges, Peaches, Pears [small]					
full requirement	½ c	6	20	50	100
½ requirement	¼ c	3	10	25	50
Grapes (full requirement)	½ c	1¼ lb	4 lb	10 lb	20 lb
½ requirement	¼ c	10 oz	2 lb	5 lb	10 lb
Frozen					
Melon balls, frozen full requirement	½ c	1½ lb	4 lb 10 oz	11 lb 8 oz	23 lb
½ requirement	¼ c	12 oz	2 lb 5 oz	5 lb 12 oz	11 lb 8 oz
Strawberries, sliced full requirement	½ c	1¾ lb	5 lb 10 oz	14 lb 2 oz	28 lb 4 oz
½ requirement	¼ c	14 oz	2 lb 13 oz	7 lb 1 oz	14 lb 2 oz
Juice, 100% Fruit full requirement	½ c	3 c	2 ½ qt + 1 c	1½ gal + 2 c	3 gal
½ requirement	¼ c	1½ c	1 qt. + ½ c	3 qt + 1 c	1½ gal
MEAT OR MEAT ALTERNATE					
Cheese, natural-snack requirement	½ oz	3 oz	10 oz	1 lb 9 oz	3 lb 2 oz
Chicken, whole excluding neck and giblets,					
lunch/supper requirement	1½ oz	1 lb 10 oz	5 lb 5 oz	13 lb 4 oz	26 lb 7 oz